BOOKKEEPING BASICS FOR SMALL BUSINESS

A BEGINNER'S GUIDE TO STRESS-FREE BOOKKEEPING (EVEN IF YOU HATE NUMBERS)

CHRISTOPHER ROMAN

CONTENTS

Introduction 7

1. LAYING THE GROUNDWORK 9
   - 1.1 Understanding the Purpose of Bookkeeping: What It Is and Why It Matters 10
   - 1.2 Key Bookkeeping Terminology Demystified 11
   - 1.3 Overcoming the "I'm Not a Numbers Person" Syndrome 13
   - 1.4 The Accounting Equation Made Easy 15
   - 1.5 How Bookkeeping Differs from Accounting 17
   - 1.6 Common Bookkeeping Mistakes to Avoid 19
2. SETTING UP YOUR BOOKKEEPING SYSTEM 21
   - 2.1 Choosing Between Manual and Digital Bookkeeping 21
   - 2.2 Essential Tools for Bookkeeping: What You Really Need 23
   - 2.3 Step-by-Step Guide to Setting Up Your Books 25
   - 2.4 Selecting the Right Bookkeeping Software for Your Business 27
   - 2.5 Creating an Effective Chart of Accounts 28
   - 2.6 Keeping Your Records Organized from Day One 33
3. MASTERING DAY-TO-DAY BOOKKEEPING TASKS 36
   - 3.1 Recording Transactions Accurately 36
   - 3.2 Managing Receipts and Expenses Like a Pro 38
   - 3.3 Understanding and Recording Debits and Credits 40
   - 3.4 Reconciling Your Accounts: A Simple How-To 42
   - 3.5 Handling Invoices and Payments Efficiently 43
   - 3.6 Streamlining Expense Tracking with Ease 45
4. FINANCIAL STATEMENTS MADE EASY 47
   - 4.1 The Basics of Balance Sheets: What They Tell You 47
   - 4.2 Income Statements (Profit & Loss): Understanding Your Profitability 50
   - 4.3 Cash Flow Statements: Keeping Track of Your Liquidity 53

4.4 Common Errors in Financial Statements and How to Fix Them 55
4.5 Using Statements to Drive Business Decisions 56

5. TAXATION AND COMPLIANCES SIMPLIFIED 61
5.1 Navigating Small Business Tax Obligations 61
5.2 Practical Tax Tips and Strategies for Small Businesses 63
5.3 Preparing for Tax Season Stress-Free 65
5.4 Understanding Depreciation for Tax Purposes 67
5.5 Common Tax Mistakes and How to Avoid Them 68
5.6 Staying Compliant: Legal Considerations for Bookkeepers 70

6. ENHANCING YOUR BOOKKEEPING EFFICIENCY 72
6.1 Time-Saving Bookkeeping Techniques for Busy Entrepreneurs 72
6.2 Automating Bookkeeping Tasks: What You Need to Know 74
6.3 Utilizing Templates to Stay Organized 76
6.4 Leveraging Cloud Solutions for Flexibility 78
6.5 Evaluating the Effectiveness of Your Bookkeeping System 80
6.6 Adapting Your Bookkeeping Practices as Your Business Grows 82

7. LEVERAGING BOOKKEEPING FOR STRATEGIC DECISIONS 85
7.1 Using Financial Data for Business Planning 85
7.2 Identifying Trends and Patterns in Your Financials 87
7.3 Making Informed Business Decisions with Bookkeeping Insights 89
7.4 The Importance of Regular Financial Reviews 91
7.5 Building a Financial Strategy Based on Your Bookkeeping 93

8. REAL-LIFE APPLICATIONS AND CASE STUDIES 96
8.1 Case Study: Bookkeeping for a Retail Business 96
8.2 Scenario Analysis: Freelancers and Sole Proprietors 98
8.3 Managing Finances in a Service-Based Business 100
8.4 Bookkeeping Challenges for Startups 102
8.5 Lessons from Common Bookkeeping Pitfalls 103
8.6 Success Stories: Mastering Bookkeeping Basics 105

9. EMPOWERMENT THROUGH BOOKKEEPING 108
9.1 Building Confidence in Your Bookkeeping Abilities 108
9.2 Cultivating a Positive Money Mindset 110
9.3 Continuous Learning and Improvement in Bookkeeping 112
9.4 The Future of Bookkeeping: Trends and Innovations 114

Conclusion 117
Bibliography 121

INTRODUCTION

Do you break out in a cold sweat when you hear "bookkeeping"? You're not alone. As a small business owner, you're juggling a million tasks, and the last thing you want to worry about is keeping your financial records in order. But here's the thing: bookkeeping is the backbone of your business. It's the key to understanding your financial health, making informed decisions, and achieving long-term success.

I know what you're thinking. "I'm not a numbers person. I don't have time for this. It's too complicated." Trust me, I've been there. When I started my first business, I was overwhelmed by the thought of managing my books. But over the past two decades, as I've built and grown multiple successful ventures, I've learned that bookkeeping doesn't have to be a nightmare.

That's why I wrote this book. I want to share my knowledge and experience with you, to help you overcome your fears and take control of your finances. Whether you're a freelancer, an entrepreneur, or someone looking to switch careers, this guide is designed to demystify bookkeeping and make it accessible to everyone.

You don't need a degree in accounting or a love for numbers to succeed. All you need is a willingness to learn and a desire to empower yourself. Throughout these pages, I'll walk you through the basics of bookkeeping, step by step. We'll cover everything from setting up your accounts to interpreting financial statements, all in a way that's easy to understand and apply.

You're busy, and the thought of adding another task to your plate might seem daunting. But here's the good news: investing a little time in learning bookkeeping, you'll save countless hours of stress and frustration. You'll be able to make better decisions, avoid costly mistakes, and ultimately, grow your business.

Each chapter is structured to build upon the previous one, with practical examples, real-world applications, and tools to help you put your newfound knowledge into practice. At the end of every chapter, you'll find a summary of key concepts to quickly review and reinforce what you've learned.

When you finish this book, you'll have the skills and confidence to easily tackle your bookkeeping. You'll be able to create and interpret financial statements, optimize your tax deductions, and make informed decisions based on your financial data. Most importantly, you'll have the peace of mind that comes with knowing you're in control of your financial destiny.

So, whether you're just starting or you've been in business for years, this book is your guide to stress-free bookkeeping. It's time to conquer your fears, take charge of your finances, and unlock your business's full potential. Let's get started on this transformative journey together.

1

LAYING THE GROUNDWORK

Tax season is approaching, and you're buried under a pile of receipts and bank statements. It's well past midnight, and the numbers are starting to blur. You meant to get ahead of your bookkeeping weeks ago, but life had other plans. With the deadline looming, that familiar sense of stress is setting in. Sound familiar? You're not alone. Many small business owners and freelancers are in similar situations, overwhelmed by the thought of managing their financial records. But what if I told you that bookkeeping doesn't have to be a source of stress? With a solid foundation, you can turn a stack of paperwork into a clear financial picture, allowing you to make informed decisions and take advantage of expansion opportunities.

With over 20 years of experience in accounting and entrepreneurship, I've witnessed firsthand how effective bookkeeping goes beyond compliance—it's a powerful tool for financial success. It's about gaining control over your financial destiny. I've written this book to guide you through the process, step by step, and to show you that even if you hate numbers, you can achieve mastery over them. You don't need advanced degrees or an affinity for spreadsheets. You just need the willingness to learn and the right tools to help you along the way.

1.1 UNDERSTANDING THE PURPOSE OF BOOKKEEPING: WHAT IT IS AND WHY IT MATTERS

At its core, bookkeeping is the systematic recording of financial transactions. This includes sales, purchases, receipts, and payments made by an individual or organization. Accurately recording these transactions ensures a clear and transparent record of your financial activities. This process ensures that every dollar is accounted for and your financial information is organized and accessible. Consider bookkeeping the foundation upon which your entire financial house is built. Without it, your business can quickly become chaotic and unmanageable.

Accurate bookkeeping is crucial for several reasons. It supports effective financial management and decision-making by providing you with a detailed overview of your financial situation. This clarity allows you to confidently prepare for tax season, ensuring that you claim every deduction you're entitled to. It also enables you to track cash flow, which is the lifeblood of any business. By monitoring the inflow and outflow of money, you can anticipate financial challenges and act proactively to mitigate them.

Failing to maintain accurate bookkeeping can lead to significant consequences. Incorrect financial reporting can distort your business's performance, resulting in poor decisions and possible legal complications. Missed tax deductions can result in paying more taxes than necessary, eating into your profits. Inadequate cash flow management can leave you scrambling to cover expenses or missing out on lucrative opportunities due to a lack of funds. In short, neglecting bookkeeping can jeopardize your business's financial health and stability.

Organized financial records do more than keep you compliant with regulations; they reveal opportunities for growth and expansion. A clear view of your finances lets you pinpoint cost-saving strategies that enhance efficiency and boost profitability. You can also plan for future investments and be ready for success. This strategic insight is invaluable for any business owner looking to thrive in a dynamic marketplace.

Contrary to popular belief, bookkeeping doesn't have to be complex or overwhelming. Simple record-keeping systems and step-by-step processes can make the task manageable, even for those who consider themselves "not numbers people." This book aims to break down the process into digestible pieces, guiding you through each step with practical examples and straightforward explanations. By the time you finish reading, you'll have the knowledge and confidence to handle your bookkeeping easily and efficiently.

1.2 KEY BOOKKEEPING TERMINOLOGY DEMYSTIFIED

In the bookkeeping world, terms like "accounts receivable" and "liabilities" can sound daunting, but they're much more straightforward than they appear. Think of accounts receivable as the money owed to your business—like when a friend borrows twenty dollars and promises to pay you back next week. It's money you expect to receive but haven't yet. Conversely, accounts payable is what your business owes to others. Imagine you've ordered supplies for your business and agreed to pay the vendor next month. That's your accounts payable, reflecting obligations yet to be fulfilled. Understanding these terms is crucial for keeping track of your business's financial health.

Next, let's tackle assets and liabilities. Assets encompass everything your business owns that has value, such as cash, equipment, or inventory. Consider your assets like a personal savings account—the more you have, the more financially secure you feel. Liabilities, however, are akin to personal loans. They represent debts or obligations your business must settle, such as loans or unpaid invoices. By balancing assets and liabilities, you gain a clear picture of your business's net worth, helping you make informed financial decisions.

The general ledger might sound complex, but it's essentially your business's financial diary. This ledger records every financial transaction, providing a comprehensive view of your business's cash flow.

The process of bank reconciliation is critical here. It involves comparing your ledger's records with your bank statements to ensure accuracy, like balancing your checkbook at the end of the month.

A chart of accounts is a structured list of all the accounts in your general ledger, each assigned a unique number. This chart helps you categorize financial transactions, making generating reports and tracking financial performance easier. Think of it as a filing cabinet with labeled folders, each representing a different category of your business's finances.

The understanding of your financial statements is crucial for any business owner. For instance, the profit and loss statement summarizes your expenses and revenues over a specific period, revealing whether your business is profitable. The cash flow statement, on the other hand, tracks how money moves in and out of your business, which helps you manage liquidity and plan for future expenses.

Debits and credits can be confusing, but they're fundamental to bookkeeping. Simply put, a debit increases asset or expense accounts, while a credit increases liability or equity accounts. It's a balancing act that ensures your books are accurate and complete.

Glossary of Key Terms

To make things easier, here's a quick glossary of key terms to reference as you delve deeper into bookkeeping:

- **Accounts Receivable**: Money owed to your business by customers.
- **Accounts Payable**: Money your business owes to suppliers, vendors or creditors.
- **Assets**: Valuable resources owned by your business.
- **Balance Sheet**: A financial statement that shows a snapshot of a company's financial position at a specific point in time. It lists the company's assets, liabilities, and equity.
- **Bank Reconciliation**: The process of matching the balances

in a business's accounting records to the corresponding bank statement.

- **Cash Flow Statement**: A report tracking cash movement in and out of your business.
- **Chart of Accounts**: A list of all accounts used in the general ledger, organized by category (e.g., assets, liabilities, income, expenses).
- **Debits and Credits**: Entries that increase or decrease accounts in double-entry bookkeeping.
- **Expense**: Costs incurred in the process of earning revenue (e.g., rent, salaries, utilities).
- **General Ledger**: A record of all financial transactions within your business.
- **Liabilities**: Debts or obligations your business must repay.
- **Profit and Loss Statement**: A report detailing your business's revenues and expenses.

By demystifying these terms and concepts, you empower yourself to handle your business's finances confidently. Understanding the language of bookkeeping opens the door to better financial management and decision-making, setting the stage for success.

1.3 OVERCOMING THE "I'M NOT A NUMBERS PERSON" SYNDROME

Many people recoil at the thought of numbers, often branding themselves as "not a math person." This self-imposed label can create a mental block, leading to avoidance rather than engagement. Yet, bookkeeping is not about complex mathematical equations or abstract theories. It's about practical, day-to-day financial management. The fear of numbers often stems from misconceptions about what bookkeeping involves. Instead of intimidating calculations, it focuses on simple arithmetic and logical organization. You can gradually build confidence by breaking down these tasks into small, manageable parts. The goal is not to transform you into a mathematician but to empower you with the skills to manage your finances effectively.

Adopting a growth mindset can radically change your perspective on bookkeeping. This mindset embraces the idea that abilities can be developed through dedication and hard work. It encourages you to view challenges as opportunities for growth. With bookkeeping, practice and repetition are your allies. Start by setting achievable goals, such as reconciling your accounts monthly or categorizing expenses weekly. As you accomplish these tasks, you'll notice your confidence growing. Celebrate these small victories! They are stepping stones to mastering more complex bookkeeping tasks. Consistent practice will improve your skills and reduce anxiety over time. Remember, every expert once started as a beginner, and you can achieve proficiency with perseverance.

Practical strategies can help you navigate the fear of handling financial data. Begin by breaking tasks into smaller, less daunting steps. Instead of tackling a year's worth of receipts at once, set aside a few minutes daily to update your records. Use simple tools like calculators or budgeting apps to simplify calculations. Recognize the progress you make, no matter how minor it seems. Each step forward is a component in constructing a solid foundation of financial literacy. Sharing your journey with peers or mentors can provide support and motivation. You may find encouragement and tips from others who have walked the same path, reinforcing that you're not alone in this endeavor.

Consider the story of a freelancer who initially struggled with bookkeeping due to a fear of numbers. By breaking down tasks into smaller components, this individual gradually gained confidence. Over time, that initial anxiety transformed into competence, allowing the freelancer to manage their finances independently. Another example is of an entrepreneur who felt overwhelmed by the bookkeeping demands of a growing business. Through consistent practice and setting small, achievable goals, they reduced their bookkeeping anxiety and improved their financial management skills. These stories illustrate that overcoming fear is possible, and that success in bookkeeping is attainable with dedication and effort.

Visual Element: Exercises to Build Numeric Confidence

To reinforce your learning and boost numeric confidence, try these practical exercises: Start by tracking your daily expenses for a week. Use a simple spreadsheet to categorize each transaction. Another exercise is to practice calculating percentages by determining sales tax on purchases or discounts during shopping trips. These real-world applications will enhance your comfort with numbers. If you're comfortable with technology, explore budgeting apps that automate calculations, allowing you to focus on data entry and analysis. Engage in these exercises regularly, and you'll find that the stigma surrounding numbers gradually diminishes and is replaced by a newfound sense of capability and empowerment.

SMALL BUSINESS DAILY EXPENSE TRACKER

Date	Vendor	Description	Amount	Total

1.4 THE ACCOUNTING EQUATION MADE EASY

Understanding the accounting equation is like unlocking the secret code to your business's financial health. At its core, the equation is simple: Assets = Liabilities + Equity. It's the foundation of all accounting practices and a starting point for organizing your financial records. Think of assets as what your business owns, from cash to equipment, while liabilities are what your business owes, like loans or unpaid bills. Equity represents the owner's claim after liabilities are settled. This equation balances your financial world, ensuring every transaction is accounted for and your bookkeeping is in order. Imagine a seesaw where assets sit on one side and liabilities plus equity on the other. The seesaw must balance for your financial records to be accurate. When assets increase, perhaps from buying new equipment, the other side must also adjust, either by increasing liabilities if you purchased on credit or decreasing equity if you paid with cash. This balance ensures clarity and accuracy in financial reporting, guiding you in preparing financial statements and making informed business decisions.

Now, let's explore practical scenarios where the accounting equation comes into play. Picture this: you decide to purchase office supplies on credit. This transaction increases your assets because you now own more supplies, but it also increases your liabilities since you owe the supplier. On the flip side, consider receiving payment for services rendered. Your assets increase as cash enters your business, and equity rises because your work added value to the business. These everyday scenarios demonstrate how the accounting equation operates, ensuring that your records reflect every financial move accurately. The equation's brilliance lies in its ability to capture the dual nature of transactions, maintaining balance and integrity in your books.

To truly grasp the accounting equation, hands-on practice is invaluable. Here's a straightforward exercise: Calculate equity by using given assets and liabilities. Suppose your business owns $50,000 in assets and owes $20,000 in liabilities. Plug these numbers into the equation: Equity = Assets - Liabilities. In this case, Equity equals $30,000. This exercise reinforces the concept that equity is what's left for you after settling all debts. Another helpful practice is identifying missing components in financial scenarios. For instance, if you know your assets and equity but need to find liabilities, rearrange the equation: Liabilities = Assets - Equity. These exercises solidify your understanding, allowing you to apply the accounting equation confidently in real-world situations.

The importance of the accounting equation cannot be overstated. It serves as a reliable guide for maintaining accuracy in your financial records. Ensuring every transaction is balanced prevents discrepancies and errors that could undermine your business's economic health. The equation underpins every ledger entry, every financial statement, and every decision you make based on those documents. It's a constant reminder that your business's financial activities are interconnected, each one affecting the other. Mastering this equation equips you with the ability to analyze your financial position, plan strategically, and confidently navigate the complexities of business ownership. Understanding and applying the accounting equation is not just a fundamental skill; it's an empowering tool transforming how you view and manage your business's finances.

1.5 HOW BOOKKEEPING DIFFERS FROM ACCOUNTING

When you think of bookkeeping and accounting, it's easy to lump them together, imagining a sea of numbers, spreadsheets, and financial jargon. However, while they share a common goal of financial management, they serve distinct functions. Bookkeeping is the groundwork, the meticulous process of recording each financial transaction systematically. It's akin to laying bricks; you must ensure each one is in the right place for the structure to stand firm. Bookkeeping involves recording sales, payments, purchases, and receipts; maintaining a comprehensive and accurate record of your business's transactions. Bookkeepers are the diligent record keepers, ensuring the financial data is clean, organized, and ready for scrutiny. On the other hand, accounting is more like the architect who uses these bricks to design and plan. Accountants analyze, interpret, and present this data, transforming it into meaningful insights that inform strategic business decisions. They prepare financial statements, manage audits, and provide forecasts that guide the business toward its goals.

The interdependence between bookkeeping and accounting is crucial. Without accurate and detailed bookkeeping, accounting loses its foundation. Quality bookkeeping ensures that the data accountants use is reliable and accurate, enabling them to make informed recommendations and decisions. For instance, accountants rely on precise bookkeeping records to assess financial viability and risk when a business seeks to expand. They need to know exactly where the business stands financially before advising on investments or loans. In essence, bookkeeping provides the raw data that accounting refines into strategic insights. Without this harmony, businesses risk making decisions based on incomplete or inaccurate information.

Consider the specific tasks unique to each role. A bookkeeper's day might involve recording daily transactions and documenting every financial move. They handle the reconciliation of bank statements, matching them against internal records to catch discrepancies early. This task is like a detective ensuring that the puzzle pieces fit perfectly. Meanwhile, accountants take these reconciled records and prepare detailed financial statements, like the profit and loss statement or balance sheet. They conduct audits, ensuring financial practices comply with regulations and best practices. Accountants also engage in tax planning, advising on strategies to optimize tax obligations. While bookkeeping focuses on data entry and organization, accounting emphasizes analysis and strategic planning.

A common misconception is that bookkeeping is just a simple arithmetic task, but it's more than just crunching numbers. It involves understanding the flow of financial data and ensuring accuracy in documentation. It's about creating a reliable financial narrative that reflects the day-to-day operations of a business. On the other hand, accounting requires a deeper level of analysis and interpretation. Accountants must understand complex financial regulations, interpret financial data within the broader business environment, and provide strategic advice. This distinction highlights the need for both roles, each supporting the other to achieve effective financial management.

Understanding these differences is vital for any business owner, freelancer, or aspiring financial professional. Recognizing the unique participation of bookkeeping and accounting helps you appreciate the complete financial management process. It clarifies why both roles are indispensable, ensuring your business complies with financial regulations and thrives and grows in a competitive market.

1.6 COMMON BOOKKEEPING MISTAKES TO AVOID

Picture this: you've spent hours balancing your books, feeling a sense of accomplishment, only to discover a glaring error during your next financial review. Such errors are more common than you'd think, especially when balancing the many responsibilities of running a business. One frequent pitfall is failing to reconcile accounts regularly. Reconciliation is the process of ensuring that the transactions in your books match those on your bank statements. It's like assembling a mosaic where every tile has its place. Without this regular check, discrepancies can slip through the cracks, leading to an inaccurate portrayal of your financial health. Imagine preparing a budget based on flawed data—it's like trying to find your way out of the woods with a broken compass.

Another frequent misstep is misclassifying transactions. Each transaction should be categorized correctly, whether it's an asset purchase, a liability payment, or an expense. Misclassification can lead to skewed financial reports, making understanding your business's true performance difficult. For instance, recording a loan repayment as an expense rather than a liability can inflate your expenses, reducing your apparent profitability. Though minor in isolation, such errors can accumulate, leading to significant misinterpretations of your financial data.

To avoid these pitfalls, establish a routine for regular financial audits. Reviewing your records consistently allows you to catch errors early and rectify them before they compound. This process ensures that your financial statements remain accurate and reliable. Implement clear labeling and categorization practices so every transaction finds its rightful place. A well-organized chart of accounts can simplify this process, providing a framework for consistent categorization.

Consistency is key in bookkeeping. Regular updates keep your records current and accurate, preventing minor errors from snowballing into more significant issues. Set aside time each day or week to update your books, creating a habit that becomes second nature. Consider using checklists to ensure no task is overlooked, from recording sales to reconciling accounts.

The consequences of bookkeeping errors extend beyond inaccuracies in your records. Financial misstatements can lead to misguided business decisions, such as investing in areas based on erroneous profitability figures. Moreover, inaccuracies in reporting can trigger tax penalties, compounding your financial woes. Correcting these errors can drain both time and resources that would be better spent on growing your business.

But let's not forget the brighter side. By avoiding these common mistakes, you're safeguarding your financial health and setting the stage for informed decision-making and strategic growth. When your records are accurate and up-to-date, you have a solid foundation for analyzing trends, identifying opportunities, and planning for the future.

In the world of business, vigilance pays off. By maintaining accurate and consistent records, you equip yourself with the tools to steer your company toward success. You'll find yourself confidently making decisions, knowing that your financial data reflects the accurate state of your business. As you refine your bookkeeping practices, you'll discover that the peace of mind you gain is invaluable. So, embrace the discipline of meticulous record-keeping, and watch as it transforms your financial reports and entire business management approach.

2

SETTING UP YOUR BOOKKEEPING SYSTEM

Picture yourself as an artist standing before a pristine, untouched canvas. The tools you choose, whether a classic set of brushes or a digital stylus, can dramatically shape your creation. The same goes for setting up your bookkeeping system: selecting between manual and digital methods is crucial in shaping your financial future. Each has its own merits, tailored to different kinds of business landscapes. Let's explore these options to help you decide which path suits your needs best.

2.1 CHOOSING BETWEEN MANUAL AND DIGITAL BOOKKEEPING

There's something uniquely satisfying about manual bookkeeping. It's akin to writing a letter by hand; there's a tactile connection to the work. The low cost of manual bookkeeping appeals to businesses, particularly those just starting or with straightforward financial dealings. You only need some ledgers, notebooks, or simple spreadsheets. This method allows you to dive deep into each transaction, fostering an intimate understanding of your financial movements. You're not just entering numbers; you're learning the rhythm of your business, understanding cash flow intricacies, and catching details that automation might overlook.

On the other hand, digital bookkeeping is like having a personal assistant that never takes a day off. With technology, you can automate repetitive tasks, ensuring your time is spent on strategy rather than data entry. Programs like QuickBooks or Xero offer real-time access to your financial reports, allowing you to make informed decisions at the click of a button. This method provides unparalleled efficiency and accuracy, reducing human error and freeing up valuable time. As your business grows, the scalability of digital systems becomes a significant asset, accommodating increased transaction volumes without a hitch.

Deciding between manual and digital bookkeeping should be guided by your specific circumstances. Consider the size and complexity of your business. Manual bookkeeping might suffice if you run a small food cart with limited transactions or you're in a rural or remote region with unstable internet. However, digital systems can easily handle complexity if you manage a tech startup with multiple revenue streams. Budget constraints are also factors; while manual methods are inexpensive upfront, digital solutions can offer long-term savings by streamlining operations and reducing errors. Your comfort level with technology is another determinant. If you're tech-savvy, the transition to digital may be seamless. However, manual bookkeeping could be more satisfying if you prefer a hands-on approach.

Consider the ease of use and learning curve when comparing manual and digital options. Manual methods require basic arithmetic skills and organization, which can be straightforward for many. Digital bookkeeping, while initially daunting, offers user-friendly interfaces and comprehensive support, making the learning curve manageable. Additionally, digital systems boast future growth potential, adapting to your business's evolving needs. They integrate with other business tools, enhancing efficiency and providing insights driving growth.

Interactive Element: Decision-Making Checklist

To assist you in choosing the right system, use this checklist as a guide:

- **Business Complexity**: Is your business simple or complex?
- **Budget**: How much are you willing to invest in bookkeeping?
- **Tech Comfort Level**: Are you comfortable using digital tools?
- **Scalability Needs**: Do you foresee significant business growth?
- **Time Availability**: How much time can you dedicate to bookkeeping tasks?

By reflecting on these questions, you can make a well-informed decision that aligns with your business goals. Selecting the right bookkeeping approach is not just about numbers; it's about setting the foundation for a thriving enterprise tailored to your aspirations and operations.

2.2 ESSENTIAL TOOLS FOR BOOKKEEPING: WHAT YOU REALLY NEED

When setting up your bookkeeping system, you might imagine a cluttered desk filled with papers, receipts, and ledgers. However, the process can be much more streamlined in today's digital age. At the core of your toolkit is an accounting ledger or spreadsheet software. This is where you'll record every financial transaction. It's the backbone of your financial record-keeping, providing a complete view of your business's financial health. Whether you prefer traditional ledgers or digital spreadsheets, the key is consistency in logging each sale, purchase, and payment. This consistency ensures accuracy, allowing you to see exactly where your money is coming from and where it is going.

Alongside your ledger, receipt scanners or mobile apps become invaluable. These tools allow you to digitize paper receipts quickly, reducing the clutter and ensuring you have a backup of every transaction. When tax season rolls around, you'll thank yourself for having a digital receipts repository. These apps can also categorize expenses automatically, saving you time and reducing the risk of errors. As you scan each receipt, the app can update your records in real-time, meaning fewer manual entries and more time for other tasks.

Physical documents still have their place, especially for important paperwork that needs to be kept in its original form. Filing systems, whether traditional folders or digital equivalents, help organize these documents efficiently. Think of filing systems as your personal archive. You can quickly retrieve documents when needed, whether for a tax audit or a business loan application. Organize files by category, such as invoices, contracts, and bank statements, to make retrieval swift and straightforward.

While these tools form the core of your bookkeeping arsenal, there are optional tools that can elevate your efficiency. Project management software, for example, helps track tasks and deadlines, ensuring that no bookkeeping duty falls through the cracks. It can also assist in managing budgets for specific projects, giving you a broader view of your financial commitments. Additionally, cloud storage solutions provide a secure backup of your digital files. These platforms offer peace of mind, knowing your documents are safe from physical damage or technical failures. They also allow you to access your records from anywhere, making remote work seamless.

Each tool plays a distinct role in the bookkeeping process. Your ledger is for transaction recording, the heart of your bookkeeping. Scanners and apps digitize and organize paper records, ensuring thoroughness and accuracy. Filing systems keep everything in its place, ready when needed. Project management software tracks your progress and deadlines, while cloud storage ensures everything is backed up and accessible. Together, they create a comprehensive system that supports every aspect of your bookkeeping needs.

Choosing the right tools involves evaluating your business needs. Consider the features that are most important to you. Do you need software with robust reporting capabilities, or are you more concerned with ease of use? Assess the tools' learning curve and the support available to help you get started. Some tools offer extensive tutorials and customer support, making integrating them into your daily routine easier. Cost is another factor. Although some tools may have a higher upfront cost, they can save money over time by improving efficiency and minimizing errors. Weighing these factors carefully will help you choose the right tools for your business, turning bookkeeping into a smooth and streamlined process.

2.3 STEP-BY-STEP GUIDE TO SETTING UP YOUR BOOKS

Imagine this: your business is a ship setting sail, and your bookkeeping system is the compass that will guide you through calm waters and stormy seas. Without it, you might find yourself drifting aimlessly. The first step in setting up your bookkeeping system is gathering your financial documents. This means collecting everything from sales receipts and invoices to bank statements and credit card bills. These documents are the building blocks of your financial records, providing the raw data you'll need to enter into your books. Please don't overlook the importance of these documents; they are your financial story's foundation. Organizing them at the outset saves time and headaches later.

Next, open a dedicated business bank account. This is vital for separating personal and business finances. It simplifies tracking income and expenses, ensuring a clear view of your business's financial health. Mixing personal and business funds can lead to confusion and potential legal issues, especially during tax season. A business bank account provides a professional image and can help you build a credit profile for your business. Think of it as laying a strong keel for your ship, giving stability and structure.

Accuracy is paramount from the beginning. Double-check your initial entries to ensure they reflect the correct amounts and categories. Errors made early on can get out of hand, creating more significant issues down the line. Regularly updating your records is just as crucial. Set aside time each week to review and enter transactions. This prevents backlog and ensures your financial data remains current. Regular updates also allow you to spot trends or discrepancies quickly, enabling you to address issues before they grow. This discipline is like maintaining a steady course, keeping your business on track toward its goals.

Organizing your financial data involves categorizing and sorting information systematically. A chart of accounts is an essential tool in this process. It's a comprehensive list of every account in your ledger, acting as a roadmap for recording and tracking financial transactions. Customizing this chart to fit your business needs ensures it accurately reflects your operations. Another vital practice is separating personal and business expenses. This separation simplifies tax preparation and financial analysis, clearly showing your business's performance. It's akin to plotting your course on a map, ensuring you have a clear path ahead.

Beware of common pitfalls that can disrupt your bookkeeping system. Mixing personal and business funds is a frequent mistake that leads to chaos. Keep separate accounts to avoid confusion and ensure clear records. Also, resist the temptation to delay record updates. Procrastination can result in a backlog that's difficult to manage. Maintaining a routine and updating your books consistently to prevent errors and ensure accuracy is essential. This diligence acts as regular maintenance, ensuring your business operates smoothly and efficiently.

Establishing a robust system from the start sets your business up for success. This foundation allows you to confidently navigate financial challenges, knowing your records are accurate and up-to-date. With a clear understanding of your finances, you can make informed decisions that drive growth and profitability. Your bookkeeping system is not just a record of the past; it's a tool for planning the future, guiding your business toward its destination with precision and foresight.

2.4 SELECTING THE RIGHT BOOKKEEPING SOFTWARE FOR YOUR BUSINESS

Choosing the right bookkeeping software is like picking the perfect tool for a job—it needs to fit your business like a glove. Among the most popular options are QuickBooks, FreshBooks, and Xero, each offering unique features tailored to different needs. QuickBooks stands out for its comprehensive suite of features, making it a favorite among small businesses. It provides robust invoice management and real-time financial reporting. On the other hand, FreshBooks excels with its intuitive interface and is particularly favored by freelancers and service-based businesses. It simplifies time tracking and client invoicing, ensuring you spend less time on administrative tasks and more on your core business. Then there's Xero, renowned for its seamless integration capabilities. It's a powerhouse for companies looking to connect their bookkeeping with other systems, offering strong inventory management and payroll processing options.

When evaluating these software solutions, consider both features and pricing. QuickBooks, though slightly higher in cost, provides extensive capabilities, including payroll support and inventory tracking, which may justify the investment if your business requires these features. FreshBooks offers a more budget-friendly option with tiered pricing, perfect for those who prioritize easy invoicing and expense tracking without needing advanced inventory features. Xero provides a middle ground with its scalable pricing plans, allowing you to start small and add features as needed. The required functionality should guide your decision—whether it's detailed analytics, comprehensive reporting, or a simplified user interface. Consider your budget and weigh it against the features that offer the most value to your business operations.

Another critical factor is how well the software integrates with your existing tools. Compatibility can save you time and reduce errors. For instance, syncing your bookkeeping software with payment processors like PayPal or Stripe can automate transaction entries, minimizing manual work. Integration with inventory management systems is another plus, mainly if you handle physical products. This ensures that your stock levels and accounting records are always in sync, reducing discrepancies and the risk of stockouts or overstocking. Think of integration as the glue that holds your systems together, making your business run more smoothly.

To help you decide, list the essential features your business needs. Do you require advanced reporting? Is inventory management crucial? Once you have your list, research user reviews to see how others in your industry rate the software's performance and customer support. Support can be crucial when encountering technical issues or needing help understanding a feature. Look for software with a responsive support team and accessible resources, such as tutorials or user forums, which can fast-track your learning and problem-solving.

Getting started with your chosen software involves a few key steps. Begin with the initial setup by linking your business bank accounts and importing existing financial data. This creates a seamless transition from your previous system. Spend time exploring the interface and familiarize yourself with its functions. Many providers offer training resources or tutorials—use these to get up to speed quickly. Setting up consistent workflows early can save you time and prevent headaches later. As you become more comfortable, you can explore advanced features that offer deeper insights into your business's financial health.

2.5 CREATING AN EFFECTIVE CHART OF ACCOUNTS

Envision your business as a bustling city, each transaction a vehicle navigating its streets. The chart of accounts is your road map, guiding these transactions to their appropriate destinations. This organizational tool is indispensable for categorizing financial data, facilitating accurate reporting, and simplifying expense tracking. Think of it as the backbone of your financial system. Organizing and categorizing your accounts provides a clear view of your business's financial health, making it easier to track income and expenses. This clarity provides the foundation for informed decision-making, ensuring your business's financial stability and growth.

Creating a custom chart of accounts tailored to your business needs is crucial in setting up your bookkeeping system. Start by identifying the key account categories that reflect your business operations. These categories generally include assets, liabilities, equity, income, and expenses. Each category serves a distinct purpose, capturing specific types of financial activities. You'll want to assign account numbers within these categories for easy reference. These numbers help maintain organization and facilitate quick access to information. A systematic approach ensures that every transaction finds its rightful place, making it easier to generate accurate financial reports and analyze your financial data.

Customization is the key to an effective chart of accounts. Your business is unique, and your chart should reflect its individuality. Consider adding industry-specific accounts that pertain to your operations. For instance, a construction company might include accounts for project-specific materials, while a restaurant may have categories for different types of food suppliers. As your business evolves, your chart of accounts should adapt to meet new needs. This flexibility allows you to integrate new revenue streams or expense categories without disrupting your existing system. Customization ensures that you capture the uniqueness of your operations, providing a comprehensive view of your financial landscape.

Examples of account structures can offer valuable guidance as you develop your chart. For a retail business, the chart might include detailed categories for inventory, sales, and returns, while a service-based business might focus more on labor costs and service revenue. Each business type has its own demands; your chart should reflect these differences. Additionally, consider whether a simple or detailed account setup best suits your needs. A smaller business with straightforward operations might opt for a simpler chart, while a more complex enterprise may require a detailed setup to capture its multifaceted activities. This balance between simplicity and detail ensures your chart remains functional and effective.

Visual Element: Sample Chart of Accounts Templates

To help visualize your chart of accounts, consider these templates:

- **Retail Business Template**: Includes categories for sales, cost of goods sold, inventory, and operating expenses.

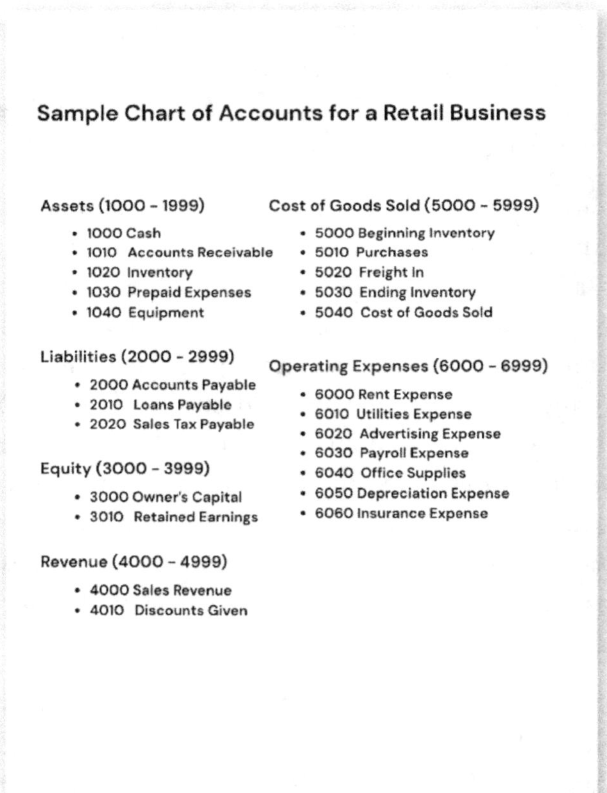

Sample Chart of Accounts for a Retail Business

Assets (1000 - 1999)

- 1000 Cash
- 1010 Accounts Receivable
- 1020 Inventory
- 1030 Prepaid Expenses
- 1040 Equipment

Liabilities (2000 - 2999)

- 2000 Accounts Payable
- 2010 Loans Payable
- 2020 Sales Tax Payable

Equity (3000 - 3999)

- 3000 Owner's Capital
- 3010 Retained Earnings

Revenue (4000 - 4999)

- 4000 Sales Revenue
- 4010 Discounts Given

Cost of Goods Sold (5000 - 5999)

- 5000 Beginning Inventory
- 5010 Purchases
- 5020 Freight In
- 5030 Ending Inventory
- 5040 Cost of Goods Sold

Operating Expenses (6000 - 6999)

- 6000 Rent Expense
- 6010 Utilities Expense
- 6020 Advertising Expense
- 6030 Payroll Expense
- 6040 Office Supplies
- 6050 Depreciation Expense
- 6060 Insurance Expense

- **Service-Based Business Template**: Focuses on service revenue, labor costs, and contract expenses.

Sample Chart of Accounts for a Service-Based Business

Assets (1000 - 1999)

- 1000 Cash
- 1010 Accounts Receivable
- 1020 Prepaid Expenses
- 1030 Office Equipment
- 1040 Software & Licenses

Liabilities (2000 - 2999)

- 2000 Accounts Payable
- 2010 Credit Card Payable
- 2020 Loans Payable
- 2030 Payroll Liabilities

Equity (3000 - 3999)

- 3000 Owner's Capital
- 3010 Retained Earnings

Revenue (4000 - 4999)

- 4000 Service Revenue
- 4010 Consulting Fees
- 4020 Retainer Fees
- 4030 Other Income

Cost of Goods Sold (5000 - 5999)

- 5000 Salaries & Wages
- 5010 Contract Labor
- 5020 Employee Benefits
- 5030 Software & Tools for Service Deliver
- 5040 Travel & Client Meetings

Operating Expenses (6000 - 6999)

- 6000 Rent & Utilities
- 6010 Office Supplies
- 6020 Marketing/Advertising
- 6030 Professional Fees
- 6040 Insurance
- 6050 Training & Development

- **Simple Setup**: Basic categories for small businesses, such as income, expenses, and net profit.

Sample Chart of Accounts for Basic Small Business/Simple

Assets (1000 - 1999)

- 1000 Cash
- 1010 Accounts Receivable
- 1020 Equipment

Liabilities (2000 - 2999)

- 2000 Accounts Payable
- 2010 Loans Payable

Equity (3000 - 3999)

- 3000 Owner's Capital
- 3010 Retained Earnings

Revenue (4000 - 4999)

- 4000 Sales/Service Revenue
- 4010 Other Income

Expenses (5000 - 5999)

- 5000 Rent
- 5010 Utilities Expense
- 5020 Payroll Expense
- 5030 Office Supplies
- 5040 Marketing/Advertising
- 5050 Insurance Expense
- 5060 Professional Fees

- **Detailed Setup**: Extensive categories for larger businesses, including sub-accounts for specific departments or projects.

Sample Chart of Accounts for Larger Business

Assets (1000 - 1999)

Current Assets

- 1000 Cash & Bank Accounts
  - 1001 Checking Account
  - 1002 Savings Account
  - 1003 Petty Cash
- 1100 Accounts Receivable
- 1200 Inventory
  - 1201 Raw Materials
  - 1202 Finished Goods

Fixed Assets

- 1500 Property, Plant & Equipment
  - 1501 Buildings
  - 1502 Machinery & Equipment
  - 1503 Vehicles
- 1600 Accumulated Depreciation

Liabilities (2000 - 2999)

Current Liabilities

- 2000 Accounts Payable
- 2100 Credit Cards
- 2200 Payroll Liabilities
- 2300 Sales Tax Payable

Long-Term Liabilities

- 2500 Loans Payable

Equity (3000 - 3999)

- 3000 Common Stock
- 3100 Retained Earnings

Revenue (4000 - 4999)

- 4000 Sales Revenue
- 4100 Service Revenue
- 4200 Interest Income
- 4300 Other Income

Cost of Goods Sold (5000 - 5999)

- 5000 Raw Material
- 5100 Direct Labor
- 5200 Manufacturing Overhead
- 5300 Freight & Shipping

Expenses (6000 - 6999)

General & Administrative

- 6000 Salaries & Wages
- 6100 Rent & Utilities
- 6200 Office Supplies
- 6300 Depreciation & Amortization

Sales & Marketing

- 6400 Advertising & Marketing
- 6500 Travel & Entertainment

Research & Development

- 6700 R & D Materials
- 6800 Product Testing

These templates provide a starting point, allowing you to customize your chart to fit your specific needs. They serve as a practical guide, helping you structure your financial data to support efficient bookkeeping and insightful analysis.

2.6 KEEPING YOUR RECORDS ORGANIZED FROM DAY ONE

Visualize yourself entering an office where papers are stacked haphazardly and important documents are scattered across desks. It's chaotic, and finding what you need can feel like searching for a needle in a haystack. Effective document organization is crucial to avoiding such chaos in your bookkeeping. One of the first steps is to implement a consistent filing system. Whether you prefer physical files or digital folders, consistency is key. Label each file or folder clearly, using categories such as invoices, receipts, or tax documents. This practice ensures that you can do so quickly and efficiently when trying to find a specific document. Separating personal and business finances is another fundamental practice. Mixing them, especially when running a small business, is tempting, but keeping them distinct avoids confusion and potential legal issues.

Consider the storage options available to you: digital versus physical. Digital storage solutions, like cloud services, offer several advantages. They provide accessibility from anywhere, allowing you to access your files even when you're not in the office. Imagine the convenience of retrieving a document from your phone during a meeting. Cloud storage also offers robust security features, protecting your files from loss due to physical damage. On the other hand, physical filing cabinets have their place, especially for original documents that must be retained in hard copy. They're simple, no tech skills required, and can be a cost-effective solution for those who prefer a tangible filing system. The decision often depends on your comfort with technology and the nature of your business documents.

Retrieving documents swiftly is vital to maintaining efficiency. A well-organized system with clear labeling is a must. For digital files, use indexing systems and digital tagging to categorize and sort documents. This approach is akin to having a library catalog; it allows you to search for documents using keywords, making retrieval almost instant. A similar system using color-coded labels or tabs can be effective for physical documents. The goal is to minimize the time spent searching, allowing you to focus on more critical tasks.

No matter how organized you are, backups are non-negotiable. Data loss can occur due to technical failures, natural disasters, or even human error. Regular digital backups protect you from such scenarios, ensuring you always have a copy of your critical documents.

Consider using automated backup solutions that schedule regular backups without requiring your intervention. This set-it-and-forget-it approach ensures continuity without adding to your workload. For physical documents, consider offsite storage solutions. This means keeping copies or originals in a separate location, safeguarding them against local hazards like fire or theft. Think of backups as your safety net, providing peace of mind that your business's financial records are secure.

As you build your bookkeeping system, remember that organization is more than neatness. It's about creating a structure supporting your business goals, ensuring you can find and use your financial data effectively. With a robust system in place, you're not just protecting your information; you're laying the groundwork for informed decision-making and strategic growth. This approach connects all the pieces of your business, from daily operations to long-term planning, creating a cohesive picture of your financial health.

3

MASTERING DAY-TO-DAY BOOKKEEPING TASKS

Let's say you're running your business and everything is running smoothly. You've got customers flowing in, your products or services are in demand, and you're finally gaining momentum. But then, at the end of the month, you sit down to review your finances and realize something doesn't add up. It's a common scenario faced by many small business owners and freelancers. The culprit? Inaccurate transaction recording. This chapter dives into the essentials of managing those daily transactions effectively. It's about establishing a routine that keeps your financial records accurate, timely, and aligned with your business goals.

3.1 RECORDING TRANSACTIONS ACCURATELY

The importance of recording transactions promptly cannot be overstated. Imagine your financial records as a diary of your business's life. Each entry you make captures a snapshot of your financial health at that moment. Recording transactions daily ensures that these snapshots are complete and reflect the true nature of your business activities. This practice prevents discrepancies that can arise from forgotten details or misplaced receipts. Maintaining a chronological order creates a clear trail of your business's financial journey, making it easier to analyze trends, prepare for tax season, and make informed decisions.

Categorizing transactions correctly is equally vital. Your chart of accounts serves as the framework for this categorization, providing predefined categories that align with your business operations. Assigning transactions to the correct categories helps maintain consistency in your financial records, ensuring that each expense and revenue source is accurately represented. Regularly reviewing and adjusting these categories is a smart practice. As your business evolves, so might your financial activities, requiring new categories or adjustments to existing ones. This flexibility ensures that your records remain relevant and reflect your current business landscape.

Technology plays a pivotal role in enhancing the accuracy of transaction recording. Mobile apps enable you to record transactions on the go, capturing details as they happen. This immediacy reduces the risk of forgetting important information and helps keep your records up-to-date. Automated bank feeds simplify this process by importing transactions directly into your accounting software. These tools streamline data entry, reduce manual errors, and save time, allowing you to focus on growing your business rather than getting bogged down in paperwork.

Despite the efficiencies technology offers, it's crucial to double-check entries to maintain accuracy. Cross-referencing your records with bank statements is fundamental in ensuring that your financial data is correct. This practice helps identify discrepancies early, preventing them from snowballing into more significant issues. Weekly spot-checking for errors adds an extra layer of assurance, allowing you to catch mistakes that might have slipped through the cracks. These checks are essential for maintaining the integrity of your financial records, providing you with reliable data for decision-making.

Interactive Element: Weekly Transaction Review Checklist

Creating a routine for reviewing your transactions can enhance accuracy and keep your records pristine. Here's a simple checklist to guide your weekly review:

- **Verify Daily Entries**: Ensure all transactions from the past week are recorded.
- **Cross-Reference with Bank Statements**: To catch discrepancies, align your entries with bank records.
- **Check for Misclassifications**: Review categories to ensure transactions are correctly assigned.
- **Spot-Check for Errors**: Randomly select entries to verify accuracy and completeness.
- **Adjust Categories as Needed**: Modify your chart of accounts to reflect any new financial activities.

Incorporating this checklist into your routine reinforces the practices that keep your financial records accurate and trustworthy. This diligence safeguards your business against financial missteps and gives you the insights to make strategic decisions.

3.2 MANAGING RECEIPTS AND EXPENSES LIKE A PRO

Receipts are the unsung heroes of bookkeeping. They're more than just scraps of paper; they're proof of your business activities. Keeping receipts is vital for accurate expense tracking and tax compliance. Imagine them as puzzle pieces, each adding to the complete picture of your business's financial health. In the event of a tax audit, receipts serve as your first line of defense, validating the expenses claimed on your tax returns. Without them, you risk facing penalties or having deductions disallowed. They also play a crucial role in expense validation, ensuring that every transaction you record is backed by tangible evidence.

Consider adopting a dual approach incorporating physical and digital systems to organize your receipts. For physical receipts, categorized folders can be your best friend. Designate a folder for each category, such as travel, meals, and supplies, and make it a habit to file receipts immediately. This system protects them from getting lost and makes retrieval straightforward. On the digital front, receipt scanning apps can revolutionize your organization. These apps allow you to snap a photo of each receipt, automatically storing it digitally. This way, even if a physical receipt fades or gets damaged, you have a pristine digital copy. Integrating these methods ensures that your receipts are safe and accessible.

Tracking and reconciling expenses is another critical aspect of effective bookkeeping. Consistent tracking aligns your expenses with your financial goals, allowing you to identify areas for cost-saving and efficiency improvements. Establish a routine, such as weekly expense review meetings, to review each expense and record it accurately. During these meetings, tag each expense with its business purpose. This practice clarifies the nature of each transaction and aids in future analysis and reporting. By regularly examining your expenses, you clearly understand where your money is going, enabling more strategic decision-making.

To reduce errors in expense records, adhere to best practices, prioritizing accuracy and consistency. Regular audits of expense reports are invaluable. These audits provide an opportunity to spot discrepancies and address them promptly. Implementing a standardized expense policy is equally important. A clear policy dictates how expenses should be recorded, categorized, and approved, minimizing the risk of misclassification or oversight. This policy should be communicated to everyone involved in the financial processes of your business, ensuring uniformity and accountability. Establishing these practices creates a robust framework that supports accurate and reliable expense management.

Visual Element: Expense Management Checklist

To keep your expense management on track, consider using this checklist:

- **Organize Receipts**: Sort physical receipts into categorized folders and digitize them using a receipt scanning app.

- **Conduct Weekly Reviews**: Schedule regular meetings to review and reconcile expenses, ensuring they align with financial goals.
- **Tag Expenses**: Assign each expense to a business purpose to clarify its role in your financial operations.
- **Perform Regular Audits**: Audit expense reports periodically to catch errors and maintain accuracy.
- **Implement a Standardized Policy**: Establish and communicate a clear expense policy to ensure consistency and compliance.

Adopting these strategies and tools doesn't just streamline your bookkeeping; it also empowers you with the confidence to manage your business finances like a pro.

3.3 UNDERSTANDING AND RECORDING DEBITS AND CREDITS

Let's dive into the world of debits and credits. These are the building blocks of bookkeeping, forming the foundation for recording transactions. Think of debits and credits as two sides of the same coin, each playing a crucial role in maintaining balance within your accounts. When you debit an account, you increase what you own or what you've spent. This means assets and expenses go up. Conversely, credits increase what you owe, what you've earned, or your ownership stake in the business. So, liabilities, revenues, and equity accounts grow with credits. It's like maintaining a balanced diet; you want to ensure that both sides are in harmony to keep your financial health in check.

Consider a typical sale transaction. When you make a sale, you're bringing in revenue, which is credited to your accounts. Simultaneously, you receive cash or an equivalent, which is debited. This dual entry ensures that your accounting equation—assets equals liabilities plus equity—remains balanced. Similarly, when you pay a bill, you're reducing your cash, which is credited, while the expense account is debited. These transactions illustrate how debits and credits work together, similar to a scale that must remain even to reflect true financial health. Each entry is a piece of the puzzle, contributing to the overall picture of your business's financial standing.

The double-entry system is the backbone of modern accounting. It ensures that every transaction impacts at least two accounts, maintaining the balance required by the accounting equation. This method prevents errors and provides a comprehensive view of your financial activities. Imagine buying equipment for your business. This purchase increases your assets and either decreases your cash or increases your liabilities, depending on whether you paid in full or financed the purchase. The double-entry system captures both aspects, providing clarity and accuracy. Balancing debits and credits ensures that your financial records are complete and reliable, serving as a trustworthy guide for financial decision-making.

Mistakes in recording debits and credits can have significant consequences. Incorrect entries can lead to discrepancies in your financial statements, creating a ripple effect that distorts your business's financial position. These errors can go unnoticed until they cause substantial issues, such as misstated profits or inaccurate cash flow projections. In the worst-case scenario, they can trigger tax audits with severe penalties for non-compliance. Imagine the stress of facing an audit, only to discover that a simple recording error led to the discrepancy. The importance of getting it right the first time cannot be overstated.

Avoiding such pitfalls requires vigilance and attention to detail. Regularly review your entries to ensure that they're correctly classified and balanced. Consider using accounting software to automate some of these processes, reducing the risk of human error and providing a clear audit trail. This technology can flag potential issues before they escalate, allowing you to correct them promptly. Embrace the practice of double-checking your work. This habit prevents errors and reinforces your understanding of how debits and credits interact. This diligence will serve you well, ensuring that your financial records remain accurate and your business stays on solid ground.

3.4 RECONCILING YOUR ACCOUNTS: A SIMPLE HOW-TO

Imagine you are piecing together a puzzle, each piece representing a transaction in your financial records. Reconciliation is the process of fitting these pieces together to form a complete picture of your business's economic health. Reconciliation is about matching your internal records with external statements, such as bank statements, to ensure consistency and accuracy. This practice is crucial, as it confirms that the transactions recorded in your books align with those reported by your bank. Regular reconciliation helps detect discrepancies early, allowing you to address them before they escalate into more significant issues.

To conduct regular account reconciliations, start by gathering all necessary documents. This includes your bank statements and any transaction reports from your accounting software. Having these documents on hand lets you compare each transaction recorded in your books with those listed on your bank statement. As you review each transaction, mark those that match to streamline the reconciliation process. This practice ensures accuracy and enhances your understanding of your financial activities. If you encounter any discrepancies, investigate their source. It could be as simple as a typo or a missed entry, but catching these errors early prevents them from compounding.

Technology can significantly streamline the reconciliation process. Many accounting software options, such as QuickBooks and Xero, offer automated reconciliation tools. These tools can match transactions automatically, flagging any mismatches for your review. Alerts for mismatched transactions are a helpful reminder, ensuring you promptly address any inconsistencies. By leveraging these technological solutions, you reduce the manual effort involved in reconciliation, allowing you to focus on more strategic aspects of your business.

These tools not only save time but also provide a layer of assurance that your records are accurate and up-to-date.

Despite the advantages of technology, challenges during reconciliation are still common. Outstanding checks, for instance, can create temporary discrepancies. These checks have been issued but have not yet been cleared by the bank. It's essential to account for these in your records and monitor them until they clear. Similarly, bank errors, though rare, can occur. An incorrect entry by the bank can lead to mismatches between your records and the bank statement. In such cases, communication with your bank is key to resolving the error and ensuring your records remain accurate.

Reconciliation is an ongoing process that requires diligence and attention to detail. Regularly scheduled reconciliations, such as monthly reviews, ensure that your financial records are consistently accurate. This practice supports accurate financial reporting and provides a solid foundation for strategic decision-making. By maintaining consistent reconciliation practices, you gain confidence in your financial data, empowering you to make informed choices that drive your business forward. As you become more familiar with the reconciliation process, you'll find that it becomes a routine part of your financial management, providing peace of mind and clarity in your business operations.

3.5 HANDLING INVOICES AND PAYMENTS EFFICIENTLY

In the small business world, timely invoicing is not just a task—it's a critical component of maintaining healthy cash flow and ensuring client satisfaction. Imagine you've completed a project and delivered outstanding results. Now, the final step is to get paid. Sending out invoices promptly ensures that your cash flow remains steady and predictable. It's like setting a rhythm for your business operations, where delays can disrupt the entire symphony. Regular billing cycles can help establish this rhythm, creating expectations for you and your clients. Implementing automated invoicing systems can further streamline this process. These systems can automatically generate and send invoices at scheduled intervals, reducing the risk of oversight and ensuring consistent cash flow. Clients appreciate this consistency, reinforcing your professionalism and making it more likely they'll pay on time.

Creating professional invoices is an art that combines clarity and precision. A well-crafted invoice is not just a payment request; it reflects your brand and commitment to your business. Start by including clear payment terms and methods. Specify when the payment is due and acceptable forms of payment, whether credit cards, checks, or online transfers. This clarity eliminates confusion and sets clear expectations, reducing the likelihood of delayed payments. Itemize the services or products provided, detailing each line item with descriptions and costs. This transparency reassures your clients of the value they're receiving and provides a clear reference if any discrepancies arise. A professional design, complete with your logo and contact information, adds a touch of professionalism that can boost your business's credibility.

Managing accounts receivable requires a proactive approach to tracking and collecting outstanding payments. Establishing a follow-up schedule is essential. It's like setting reminders for yourself to check in on unpaid invoices, ensuring nothing slips through the cracks. A gentle nudge via email or a phone call can effectively remind clients of their obligations without straining the relationship. Offering multiple payment options can also facilitate timely payments. The more convenient it is for clients to pay, the faster you'll receive what's owed. Consider accepting various forms of payment, from traditional checks to modern digital solutions like PayPal or bank transfers. This flexibility caters to diverse client preferences, making the payment process seamless and hassle-free.

Tracking payments efficiently is crucial for maintaining an accurate picture of your financial health. Payment tracking software can be a game-changer. These tools provide real-time updates on the status of your invoices, allowing you to monitor which payments have been settled and which are still pending. Integrating these systems with your accounting software can further enhance efficiency, automatically updating your records as payments are received. This integration reduces manual data entry, minimizes errors, and ensures that your financial data is always current. It's like having a personal assistant who keeps your books in order, freeing you to focus on other aspects of your business.

Handling invoices and payments effectively sets the stage for a financially stable and thriving business. The practices outlined here aren't just about efficiency but building trust and reliability with your clients. Clients who see you're organized and professional are more likely to respect your payment terms and view your business as a valued partner.

3.6 STREAMLINING EXPENSE TRACKING WITH EASE

Efficient expense tracking is a cornerstone of sound financial management. It's about having a clear, real-time view of your spending, significantly enhancing your budget management. When expenses are tracked accurately, you can allocate resources more effectively, ensuring that funds are available for critical areas of your business. This oversight leads to better forecasting and planning, allowing you to prepare for upcoming financial needs without surprises. Furthermore, streamlined tracking simplifies tax reporting. Organized expense records will enable you to quickly identify deductible expenses, making tax preparation less stressful and more precise. This efficiency minimizes the risk of missed deductions, ensuring you only pay what you owe.

Modern technology offers a myriad of tools to make this process seamless. Expense-tracking apps that sync with your bank accounts are invaluable. They automatically import transactions, categorize expenses, and provide you with a comprehensive overview of your spending patterns. This automation reduces manual entry, saving time and reducing the potential for errors. Apps with receipt capture features are particularly useful. They allow you to snap a photo of your receipt and store it digitally, so you never have to worry about losing a paper trail. These digital records are easily searchable, making it simple to retrieve information when needed, whether for audits or financial reviews.

Setting up an expense tracking system tailored to your business needs involves several steps. Begin by defining expense categories that reflect your business operations. These categories should align with your chart of accounts, ensuring consistency across your financial records. Consider setting up alerts for unusual spending. These notifications can act as an early warning system, alerting you to potential budget overruns or unauthorized expenses. Such proactive measures ensure that you stay within budget and maintain control over your financial activities. This foresight protects your bottom line and enhances your ability to respond to financial challenges.

Consistency is key to maintaining an effective expense-tracking system. Develop a habit of entering expenses daily, which keeps your records current and reduces the workload at the end of the month. Regular updates ensure that your financial data remains accurate, facilitating timely decision-making. Incorporate monthly expense reviews into your routine. These reviews offer an opportunity to analyze spending patterns, identify areas for cost-saving, and make informed adjustments to your budget. This regular assessment acts as a financial health check, ensuring your business remains on track to meet its financial goals.

Adopting these practices doesn't just streamline your bookkeeping; it empowers you with the insights needed to drive strategic growth. By maintaining accurate and up-to-date expense records, you gain a deeper understanding of your financial position, enabling you to make decisions confidently. This clarity supports everything from daily operations to long-term planning, providing a solid foundation for your business's success. As you refine your expense tracking practices, you'll discover that the peace of mind and control you gain are invaluable assets. This chapter has equipped you with the knowledge to manage your day-to-day bookkeeping tasks effectively, setting the stage for deeper financial understanding in the chapters to come.

4

FINANCIAL STATEMENTS MADE EASY

Imagine you're a detective, piecing together the clues of your business's financial story. The balance sheet is your magnifying glass, offering a close-up view of what your business owns and owes at any given moment. It's a snapshot of your financial position, revealing the assets, liabilities, and equity that define your enterprise's health. Understanding this statement is like mastering the art of deciphering a map; once you know what each component signifies, you can confidently navigate the complexities of financial management.

4.1 THE BASICS OF BALANCE SHEETS: WHAT THEY TELL YOU

The balance sheet is divided into three primary sections: assets, liabilities, and equity. Assets represent what your business owns. These are split into current and non-current assets. Current assets, such as cash, accounts receivable, and inventory, are items you can convert into cash within a year. They're your business's short-term resources, the fuel that keeps daily operations running smoothly. Non-current assets, like property and equipment, are more like long-term investments. They hold value over time, contributing to the stability and growth of your business. Liabilities, on the other hand, represent what your business owes. These are categorized as short-term (current liabilities) and long-term (non-current liabilities). Current liabilities include obligations like accounts payable and short-term loans, due within a year. Long-term liabilities, such as mortgages or bonds payable, are debts due beyond a year, reflecting more enduring commitments. Equity, the third component, is the residual interest in the assets after liabilities are deducted, representing the owner's claim on the business.

The balance sheet equation, Assets = Liabilities + Equity, is the foundation that keeps this financial puzzle intact. This equation ensures that every transaction is balanced, maintaining the integrity of your financial records. For instance, your assets increase when you purchase new equipment. If you financed it with a loan, your liabilities increase correspondingly, maintaining balance. This interconnectedness provides a clear picture of how your business resources are funded and utilized, offering a comprehensive view of your financial standing.

A balance sheet serves multiple purposes, offering insight into your business's liquidity and financial stability. Liquidity refers to your ability to meet short-term obligations, a crucial indicator of financial health. By comparing current assets to current liabilities, you can assess whether you have enough resources to cover immediate expenses. This assessment is vital for planning cash flow and avoiding financial shortfalls. Evaluating financial stability involves examining the proportion of assets funded by debt versus equity. A balance sheet helps you understand this balance, highlighting potential risks and opportunities for growth.

In practical terms, balance sheets are invaluable tools for decision-making and financial planning. Determining your net worth is one such use, providing a measure of your business's equity after all liabilities are settled. This process is a key indicator of financial success, guiding strategic decisions. Planning for financial growth is another critical application. By analyzing assets and liabilities, you can identify areas for investment or cost reduction, paving the way for expansion and increased profitability.

To illustrate, consider a small business with assets totaling $150,000, liabilities of $80,000, and equity of $70,000. This simple snapshot reveals the business's financial condition, showing owners have a $70,000 stake after settling debts—such clarity aids in evaluating performance, attracting investors, and securing loans. A well-prepared balance sheet speaks volumes, providing a transparent account of your business's financial health and guiding informed decisions. Understanding its intricacies empowers you to steer your business toward a prosperous future.

Visual Element: Sample Balance Sheet (Assets, Liabilities and Equity)

This example of a balance sheet shows the basic layout between assets, liabilities and equity.

XYX COMPANY
Balance Sheet
12/31/2024

ASSETS	
Current Assets:	
Cash	$12,000
Accounts Receivable	$35,000
Inventory	$120,000
Prepaid Rent	$8,000
Total Current Assets:	$175,000
Long-Term Assets:	
Land	$126,000
Buildings & Improvements	$300,000
furniture & Fixtures	$50,000
General Equipment	$125,000
Total Long-Term Assets:	$601,000
TOTAL ASSETS	$776,000
LIABILITIES	
Current Liabilities:	
Accounts Payable	$60,000
Taxes Payable	$25,000
Salaries/Wages Payable	$30,000
Interest Payable	$25,000
Total Current Liabilities:	$140,000
Long-Term Liabilities:	
Loan 1	$322,000
Total Long-Term Liabilities:	$322,000
TOTAL LIABILITIES	$462,000
OWNER'S EQUITY	
Paid in Capital	$64,000
Retained Earnings	$250,000
TOTAL OWNER'S EQUITY	$314,000
TOTAL LIABILITIES & OWNER'S EQUITY	$776,000

4.2 INCOME STATEMENTS (PROFIT & LOSS): UNDERSTANDING YOUR PROFITABILITY

An income statement, often called a profit and loss (P&L) statement, is like the heartbeat of your business, recording the rhythm of revenue and expenses over a specific period. It summarizes how money flows in and out, highlighting the profitability of your enterprise. At its core, this statement breaks down revenue streams, categorizing them into operating and non-operating revenues. Operating revenue comes from primary business activities, such as sales of products or services. Non-operating revenue, however, might arise from secondary sources like interest earned or asset sales, providing additional insight into cash inflow. On the other side, expenses are split into operational and non-operational categories as well. Operational expenses cover the costs directly associated with running the business, from salaries to rent and utilities. Non-operational expenses might include one-time costs such as legal fees or restructuring charges, offering a comprehensive view of outflows.

Each section of this statement is significant. Gross profit, the difference between revenue and the cost of goods sold, highlights the efficiency of your production and sales processes. It's the initial marker of how well your core operations are performing. Operating profit, which deducts operating expenses from gross profit, digs deeper. It shows how well your business manages its day-to-day expenses and operations. Net profit, or the bottom line, is what's left after all expenses, taxes, and interest. This figure directly reflects profitability, showing what truly contributes to growth or loss. Understanding these margins is crucial, as they reveal the impact of cost control measures on overall profitability. For instance, tightening control on expenses without sacrificing quality can lead to higher net profits, a sign of effective management.

Analyzing profitability trends over time helps you craft strategies and anticipate challenges. By comparing year-on-year data, you can identify growth patterns or potential declines. This comparison acts as a compass, guiding you toward informed strategic planning. For instance, if you notice a consistent increase in operating expenses, it may signal a need to review and streamline operations. This process helps uncover cost reduction opportunities, such as negotiating better supplier contracts or automating costly manual processes. These powerful insights enable you to make proactive decisions that enhance profitability and sustainability.

Visual Element: Sample Income Statement (Profit & Loss)

Here is an example of a profit and loss/income statement.

XYX COMPANY
Profit & Loss
January through December 2024

	Jan - Dec 24
Ordinary Income/Expense	
Income	
Sale of Product	33,255.59
Services	61,313.49
Total Income	94,569.08
Cost of Goods Sold	
Cost of Goods Sold	38,579.00
Total Cost of Goods Sold	38,579.00
Gross Profit	55,990.08
Expense	
Advertising & Marketing	1621.55
Credit Card Fees	2233.42
Dues & Subscriptions	1244.01
Job Supplies	7111.00
Legal & Professional Services	535.00
Meals & Entertainment	164.65
Office Supplies & Software	277.58
Postage & Delivery	223.98
Utilities	1702.01
Total Expense	22,463.19
Net Ordinary Income	33,526.19
Other Income/Expense	
Other Income	
Sales Tax Adjustment	62.98
Total Other Income	62.98
Net Other Income	62.98
Net Income	33,589.87

This snapshot provides a clear picture of the business's financial health, showing where money is made and spent. Visual aids like graphs can depict these trends over time, illustrating revenue and expense shifts and giving a clear view of financial momentum. Graphs offer an immediate, intuitive understanding of where the business is heading, allowing for swift adjustments to strategy.

4.3 CASH FLOW STATEMENTS: KEEPING TRACK OF YOUR LIQUIDITY

Think of the cash flow statement as a dynamic snapshot of your business's financial pulse, revealing the rhythm of cash coming in and going out. Unlike other financial statements focusing on profitability or financial position, this statement sheds light on liquidity—your business's capacity to fulfill short-term obligations and maintain operations. The cash flow statement is divided into three critical sections: operating activities, investing activities, and financing activities. Operating activities encompass the core business transactions, such as cash received from customers and cash paid to vendors or suppliers. This section paints a picture of how well your business generates cash from its primary operations. Investing activities detail cash used or generated from asset investments, such as purchasing equipment or selling property. It provides insight into strategic growth moves and long-term viability. Lastly, financing activities outline cash flows related to borrowing and repaying debt, as well as equity transactions. This section tells the story of how your business raises capital and returns value to shareholders.

Understanding the distinction between cash flow and profit is crucial. Profit, as reported on the income statement, reflects your business's overall financial performance over a period of time. However, it doesn't always equate to cash on hand. For instance, you might report high profits but face cash shortages if customers delay payments. On the other hand, cash flow tracks the actual movement of cash, offering a more immediate view of liquidity. This distinction is vital for managing day-to-day operations and planning for future financial needs. A healthy cash flow ensures you can pay employees, settle debts, and invest in growth opportunities without external financing.

Creating a cash flow statement involves a structured approach. You can choose between the direct and indirect methods for reporting cash flow from operations. The direct method documents cash receipts and payments, providing a straightforward view of cash transactions. It lists cash collected from customers, cash paid to suppliers, and other cash disbursements. The indirect method, however, starts with net income and adjusts for non-cash items and changes in working capital. This approach reconciles net income to cash flow, highlighting how operating activities affect cash. Adjustments for non-cash transactions, such as depreciation, are crucial. They ensure that your cash flow statement reflects actual cash movements, not just accounting entries.

Interpreting cash flow trends involves analyzing patterns to predict future cash needs. Identifying cash surpluses and deficits is the first step. A surplus indicates excess cash, allowing you to invest or save. A deficit signals a need to secure additional funding or cut expenses. Seasonal cash flow variation analysis is equally important, especially for businesses with fluctuating demand. Understanding these cycles helps you prepare for lean periods by building cash reserves during peak seasons. This forward-looking approach ensures that your business remains resilient, even in the face of unexpected obstacles and challenges.

Consider a sample cash flow statement for a small business. In this example, the company reports $150,000 from operating activities, driven by robust sales and efficient expense management. Investing activities show a cash outflow of $50,000, reflecting a strategic purchase of new equipment. Financing activities include a $30,000 loan repayment, reducing overall debt. The net cash flow for the period is $70,000, a positive liquidity indicator. This statement provides a straightforward narrative of cash movements, offering insights into operational efficiency and strategic investments. Commentary on changes in cash positions can further enhance understanding, highlighting key drivers behind cash inflows and outflows. This analysis offers valuable lessons, empowering you to make informed financial decisions and optimize cash management.

Interactive Element: Cash Flow Analysis Exercise

Try this exercise to deepen your understanding of cash flow analysis. Review your cash flow statement, focusing on changes in cash positions across operating, investing, and financing activities. Identify any patterns or anomalies, and consider what they reveal about your business's financial health. Are there areas where cash flow could be improved? This hands-on approach reinforces the concepts discussed, enabling you to apply them to your specific business context.

4.4 COMMON ERRORS IN FINANCIAL STATEMENTS AND HOW TO FIX THEM

In the world of financial statements, accuracy is paramount. However, errors can creep in, leading to significant consequences. One frequent slip-up is the misclassification of accounts. This occurs when expenses or revenue are placed in the wrong categories, skewing your financial picture. Imagine categorizing a long-term investment as a short-term asset; it can falsely inflate your liquidity and lead to misguided financial decisions. Similarly, inaccurate revenue recognition, where income is recorded at the wrong time, can distort your profit and loss statements. This error can give a misleading view of your company's performance, making it seem more or less successful than it truly is. Such inaccuracies aren't just numbers—they can mislead stakeholders and distort your business's financial health.

The impact of these errors extends beyond your balance sheets. Misleading financial health indicators can cause investors, creditors, and management teams to make poor decisions. For instance, if revenues are overstated, a business might appear more profitable than it actually is, leading to overconfidence and risky financial maneuvers. Conversely, understated revenues can result in missed growth opportunities due to an overly cautious approach. These errors impair strategic planning, setting your business on a course dictated by inaccurate data. With flawed information, you might allocate resources inefficiently, invest in non-performing sectors, or miss out on lucrative opportunities. The ripple effect can be extensive, affecting everything from day-to-day operations to long-term strategic goals.

Detecting and correcting these mistakes requires vigilance and a systematic approach. Regular audits and reviews of your financial statements are crucial. They act like a safety net, catching errors that could otherwise go unnoticed. By implementing a schedule for internal audits, you ensure that all entries align with actual transactions. This practice helps identify discrepancies early, allowing for prompt corrections. Establishing internal controls is another effective strategy. These controls create checkpoints in your financial processes, where data is verified before moving to the next stage. Think of it as building a series of gates each transaction must pass through, ensuring accuracy at every step. This method not only prevents errors but also enhances the reliability of your financial data.

Technology plays a vital role in preventing future errors. Modern accounting software often includes error-checking features that automatically flag inconsistencies or anomalies. These tools can alert you to potential issues before they become significant problems. Additionally, they streamline the reconciliation process, matching your records with bank statements to ensure consistency. Such software can be a game-changer, reducing the manual effort involved in error detection and freeing time for more strategic tasks. However, technology is most effective when paired with well-trained staff. Providing ongoing training on financial statement preparation ensures that every team member understands the importance of accuracy and is equipped to spot errors. This training fosters a culture of precision and accountability, where everyone takes ownership of their role in maintaining financial integrity.

By addressing these common errors proactively, you safeguard your business against the pitfalls of inaccurate financial reporting. The goal isn't just to correct mistakes when they occur but to establish a robust system that minimizes the risk of errors from the outset. It's about creating an environment where accuracy is the norm, not the exception, empowering you to make informed decisions that drive success.

4.5 USING STATEMENTS TO DRIVE BUSINESS DECISIONS

Financial statements are more than just records of past activity; they are the lenses through which you can view the future of your business. Imagine them as a toolkit, each tool designed to provide insights that guide strategic choices. When you look at these statements, you see a clear path forward, highlighting opportunities for growth and areas needing attention. They help you identify where to invest and when to hold back, offering a blueprint for expansion or consolidation. For instance, a cash flow statement might show that your business has enough liquidity to support a new product line launch. In contrast, an income statement could reveal that specific cost centers are ripe for optimization.

Using financial statements effectively involves leveraging them to form strategic plans. Think of scenario planning as a way to test various business strategies without risk. You can create models based on different financial outcomes, such as what happens if sales increase by 10% or a new competitor enters the market. These scenarios allow you to prepare for various possibilities, ensuring you're ready to pivot when necessary. Budgeting and forecasting are closely linked, providing a framework for setting financial goals and monitoring progress. By aligning your budget with historical data from your statements, you create realistic benchmarks that guide financial decision-making. This alignment ensures that your business remains on track, adjusting as needed to meet financial targets.

Yet, financial statements are not without their pitfalls. One common misinterpretation is the overreliance on a single metric. Focusing solely on profit can obscure other critical aspects of financial health, like cash flow or debt levels. A business might appear profitable while struggling to cover its short-term liabilities, which can lead to financial distress if not addressed. Ignoring external economic factors is another frequent oversight. Market trends, regulatory changes, or shifts in consumer behavior can all impact your business's financial performance. Comprehensive analysis requires considering these external influences to make informed decisions that align with expansive economic conditions.

Real-world examples illuminate how these practices translate into strategic decision-making. Consider a company that used cash flow analysis to decide on expanding its operations. By evaluating its cash flow statements, the business identified surplus funds that could be reinvested into new facilities, enabling growth without compromising financial stability. In another scenario, a business leveraged profit analysis to implement cost-cutting measures. By dissecting its income statement, the company identified high overhead costs in its logistics operations, leading to a reevaluation of supplier contracts and a subsequent reduction in expenses. These examples demonstrate the power of financial statements in shaping business strategy, offering a roadmap for success.

Understanding how to use financial statements effectively empowers you to make confident decisions. They transform abstract numbers into actionable insights, guiding your business toward its goals. As you harness the full potential of these tools, you gain a deeper understanding of your business's financial landscape, ready to seize opportunities and navigate challenges with clarity and precision.

BOOKKEEPING BASICS FOR SMALL BUSINESS:

A BEGINNER'S GUIDE TO STRESS-FREE BOOKKEEPING – EVEN IF YOU HATE NUMBERS

Hey there, aspiring Bookkeeper!

You already took the brave step of learning about bookkeeping. That's awesome! Now, I'm asking for one more small thing:

Can you help me help more people by leaving a review of the book?

It doesn't cost a thing and takes just a minute, but it can make a big difference. Your review could help:

- One more small business stay afloat.
- One more entrepreneur chase their dream.
- One more person feel less afraid of numbers.
- One more family bring in steady income.
- One more big idea come to life.

People often decide what books to read based on reviews. So your words can help someone just like you take that first step.

Want to help? Just scan the code or click here to leave a review:

[https://www.amazon.com/review/review-your-purchases/?asin=B0F881CHZW]

If you're someone who likes to lift others up, thank you—from the bottom of my heart.

You're helping turn confusion into confidence, and that means the world.

Let's make bookkeeping feel a little less scary—and a lot more doable—for everyone.

Warmly,

Christopher Roman

Author of *Bookkeeping Basics for Small Business*: *A Beginner's Guide to Stress-Free Bookkeeping – Even If You Hate Numbers*

5

TAXATION AND COMPLIANCES SIMPLIFIED

Imagine you're about to embark on a road trip. You've packed your bags, filled the tank, and mapped your route. But what if you forgot to check the weather forecast? A sudden storm could leave you stranded. Navigating taxes for your small business is much like planning that trip—without a clear understanding of the landscape, you risk facing unexpected financial storms. Taxes can seem like a complex maze, but once you understand the core obligations, they transform from intimidating obstacles into manageable tasks.

5.1 NAVIGATING SMALL BUSINESS TAX OBLIGATIONS

For small business owners, understanding tax obligations is crucial. At the federal level, income tax is a primary consideration. It involves reporting earnings and paying taxes on profits. Depending on your business structure, this might mean filing as an individual or a corporation. State income tax is another layer, varying by location, impacting how you report and calculate taxes. If you're self-employed, the self-employment tax adds another dimension, covering Social Security and Medicare contributions. Payroll taxes are essential if you have employees, including funding their Social Security and Medicare. And let's not forget sales tax, which is applicable when selling goods or services. Each tax type has its nuances, requiring careful attention to ensure compliance.

Navigating tax forms is another vital task. The form you use depends on your business's structure. Sole proprietors typically file Form 1040 with a Schedule C, detailing business income and expenses. If you've formed a corporation, you'll likely use Form 1120 for C-Corporations or Form 1120-S if you've elected S-Corporation status. Each form has its own set of rules and requirements. Freelancers and independent contractors must also consider Form 1099, which reports income received outside traditional employment. These forms are more than paperwork; they're the backbone of your tax obligations, ensuring you're reporting income accurately and taking advantage of applicable deductions.

Bookkeeping plays a critical role in tax preparation. Accurate records are essential for meeting tax requirements and maximizing deductions. When you precisely track your income and expenses, you create a transparent financial history that supports your tax filings. This transparency reassures tax authorities and stakeholders alike, reducing the risk of audits. Organizing tax documents throughout the year prevents the last-minute scramble often associated with tax season. It allows you to confidently approach tax preparation, knowing that your records are complete and accurate. Proper bookkeeping simplifies tax filings and positions you to identify potential deductions, ultimately saving money.

Understanding tax deadlines is key to avoiding penalties and interest. Tax obligations occur on both an annual and quarterly basis. Annual tax payments align with the calendar year, requiring you to file returns by a specific date, often April 15th for federal taxes. Quarterly tax payments are necessary for certain businesses, particularly those with variable income. These payments help avoid underpayment penalties by spreading your tax liability across the year. Keeping track of key filing dates is essential. Missing a deadline can result in fines and interest charges, eroding your hard-earned profits. By staying informed about these timelines, you protect your financial standing and gain peace of mind.

Visual Element: Tax Obligation Checklist

To help you stay on top of your tax responsibilities, use the following checklist:

- **Federal Income Tax**: Determine if you file as an individual or corporation.
- **State Income Tax**: Research specific requirements for your state.
- **Self-Employment Tax**: Ensure you're accounting for Social Security and Medicare.
- **Payroll Taxes**: Set up systems for employee withholdings.
- **Sales Tax**: Verify if your products/services require sales tax.
- **Tax Forms**: Identify the correct forms based on your business structure.
- **Tax Deadlines**: Mark key filing dates on your calendar to avoid penalties.

Integrating these guidelines into your business routine, you'll navigate the tax landscape more efficiently, ensuring compliance and financial success.

5.2 PRACTICAL TAX TIPS AND STRATEGIES FOR SMALL BUSINESSES

Managing taxes can feel daunting. However, with a few strategic steps, you can simplify the process and avoid unnecessary headaches. One practical approach is setting aside funds specifically for taxes in a separate account. This simple step ensures you're not caught off guard when tax payments are due. Think of it as a financial cushion that softens the blow of tax season. By regularly depositing a percentage of your earnings into this account, you create a safeguard against unexpected liabilities and ensure that you're always prepared to meet your obligations without stress.

Embracing technology can further streamline your tax management. Tax software offers a reliable way to calculate taxes accurately, reducing the risk of errors and ensuring compliance with tax regulations. These tools often have features that help you track expenses, manage deductions, and even file returns electronically. By automating these tasks, you free up valuable time and minimize the possibility of oversight. The precision offered by tax software can be particularly helpful and beneficial for small business owners juggling multiple responsibilities. It acts as a digital assistant that keeps your tax matters organized and up-to-date.

Proactive tax planning is another strategy that can significantly reduce your tax liability. You can make the most of available deductions and credits by carefully timing your income and expenses. For instance, deferring income to the following year or accelerating expenses can lower your taxable income for the current year. Additionally, utilizing retirement plans like IRAs or 401(k)s provides tax advantages while helping you save for the future. Contributions to these plans can often be deducted from your taxable income, providing a dual benefit of reducing your tax burden and securing your financial future.

In some cases, the expertise of a professional tax advisor can be invaluable. Complex tax situations, such as those involving multiple revenue streams or international transactions, may require specialized knowledge. A professional can ensure that you're compliant with current regulations and help you navigate changes in tax law. Their insights can also reveal opportunities for tax savings that you might not be aware of. Partnering with a tax advisor can provide peace of mind, knowing that your tax matters are in capable hands.

Understanding tax deductions is central to effective tax management. Deductions reduce your taxable income, leading to significant savings. They represent ordinary and necessary expenses incurred while running your business. Common deductions include office supplies and equipment costs, travel, and entertainment. Health insurance premiums are also deductible for self-employed individuals, providing a relief on personal expenses. By claiming these deductions, you can decrease your debt and retain more of your hard-earned money.

Accurate documentation is vital when claiming deductions. Always maintain detailed records of all deductible expenses, including receipts and invoices. Digital receipts and expense logs are practical tools that simplify this process. Keeping everything organized ensures you can substantiate your claims if questioned by tax authorities. This organization not only facilitates tax filing but also enhances your financial management, providing clarity on where your money is going.

Some deductions are often overlooked, such as depreciation on business equipment. This deduction allows you to spread the cost of an asset over its useful life, reducing your taxable income each year. Similarly, health insurance premiums for the self-employed can be deducted, providing additional tax relief. These missed opportunities highlight the importance of understanding and utilizing all available deductions. Doing so optimizes your tax strategy, maximizing your savings and strengthening your business's financial position.

5.3 PREPARING FOR TAX SEASON STRESS-FREE

Imagine walking through a garden, tending to plants daily, rather than trying to revive a neglected plot at the last minute. Year-round tax preparation is much the same. It involves consistent care and attention to your financial records, ensuring they remain accurate and up-to-date. Monthly reconciliation of your financial records is one way to achieve this. Regularly comparing your internal records with bank statements can catch discrepancies early, preventing them from later snowballing into more significant issues. This habit keeps your financial garden tidy, allowing you to approach tax season confidently rather than dreadfully. Regular updates to your income and expense logs also ensure that every transaction is accounted for. This consistency simplifies tax filing and provides a clear picture of your financial health throughout the year.

As tax season approaches, assembling the necessary documents becomes a priority. Consider this as gathering ingredients for a recipe; each document plays a vital role in creating your final tax return. Essential documents include income statements and balance sheets detailing your business's financial performance and position. Receipts and expense records are equally important, as they substantiate your claims for deductions and credits. Organizing these documents beforehand will streamline the filing process and reduce the likelihood of missed deductions. Consider creating a checklist to ensure that you have all the necessary paperwork at your fingertips when it's time to file. This preparation alleviates stress and allows you to focus on accurately reporting your financial activities.

Reducing tax season anxiety is achievable with a few strategic steps. Set reminders for key deadlines, such as filing dates and estimated tax payments, to avoid last-minute scrambles. These reminders act as gentle nudges, keeping you on track and ensuring that no deadlines slip by unnoticed. Allocating dedicated time for tax review and preparation is another effective strategy. By setting aside specific blocks of time in your schedule, you can tackle tax tasks without the pressure of other responsibilities weighing on you. This focused approach allows you to address tax matters thoroughly and methodically, reducing stress and enhancing accuracy.

Utilizing tools and resources can further ease the tax preparation process. Online tax calculators offer a quick and easy way to estimate your tax liability, giving you a sense of what to expect before you file. Tax preparation workshops or webinars provide valuable insights and guidance, helping you navigate the complexities of tax law. These resources enhance your understanding of tax obligations and equip you with the knowledge to manage your taxes effectively. They're like a guidebook, offering direction and clarity in the often-confusing world of taxation. By leveraging these tools, you simplify the preparation process and gain confidence in handling your tax responsibilities.

5.4 UNDERSTANDING DEPRECIATION FOR TAX PURPOSES

Think of depreciation as the gradual wear and tear of your business assets. Over time, the office furniture that once gleamed with newness or the delivery van that proudly bore your business's logo start showing signs of age. Depreciation allows you to account for this decline in value over an asset's useful life. For tax purposes, it's a powerful tool, spreading the cost of an asset over several years rather than taking the hit all at once. This method reduces your taxable income, as you essentially write off a portion of the asset's cost each year. There are various methods for calculating depreciation, but the straight-line method is the simplest. It divides the asset's cost evenly across its useful life. However, if you prefer to accelerate the deductions, options like double-declining balance allow you to take more significant deductions in the early years. This approach can be advantageous if your business needs more deductions upfront.

Let's break down how you might calculate depreciation. Suppose you purchase a piece of machinery for $10,000, with a useful life of 5 years and no salvage value. Using the straight-line method, the annual depreciation would be $2,000 ($10,000/5 years). Alternatively, let's explore the Modified Accelerated Cost Recovery System (MACRS), a favored method for flexibility and higher initial deductions. MACRS assigns a specific depreciation schedule to each asset class, often accelerating the depreciation rate in the early years. For instance, office equipment may fall under a 5-year category, while vehicles might be under 7-year schedules. This system encourages investment in new equipment by allowing businesses to recover costs rapidly, ultimately deferring tax payments and improving cash flow.

The benefits of depreciation extend beyond mere tax deductions. By reducing taxable income, you ease your tax burden, freeing up cash flow to reinvest in your business. Whether it's updating technology or expanding operations, the savings from depreciation can fund growth initiatives. Additionally, accelerated depreciation methods like MACRS can defer tax payments, giving you more control over your financial planning. This flexibility is crucial, especially for businesses experiencing fluctuating income levels. By strategically timing asset purchases and leveraging depreciation, you align tax savings with business needs, maximizing financial efficiency.

When considering which assets are eligible for depreciation, consider those items integral to your daily operations. Office furniture, from desks to ergonomic chairs, falls under this category, as do the computers and printers that keep your business connected. Vehicles used for business are also depreciable, whether delivery vans or company cars. These assets typically have a finite useful life, making them prime candidates for depreciation. Other examples might include manufacturing equipment or even certain improvements to your business property. By understanding what qualifies, you ensure you're taking full advantage of the tax benefits available, optimizing your financial strategy, and capitalizing on every opportunity to reduce your tax liability.

Interactive Element: Depreciation Example Calculation Exercise

Let's walk through an exercise using the MACRS method for a business vehicle valued at $30,000. Assume it's classified under a 5-year recovery period. For simplicity, the MACRS table indicates a first-year depreciation rate of 20%. Your first-year depreciation deduction would be $6,000 ($30,000 x 20%). Each subsequent year would follow the table's specified rates, offering a structured approach to managing asset costs. This example lets you understand how depreciation calculations influence financial planning and tax strategy.

5.5 COMMON TAX MISTAKES AND HOW TO AVOID THEM

Managing taxes can be challenging, especially for those unfamiliar with the complexities of business finances. One of the most frequent errors is submitting incorrect or incomplete tax forms. This can happen when you miss a line item or forget to attach necessary documentation. Each form has its own set of requirements, and a seemingly minor oversight can lead to significant issues. Misreporting income or expenses is another common blunder, whether an accidental overstatement or understatement. Such discrepancies skew your financial picture and raise red flags with tax authorities. These errors can prompt audits, which are time-consuming and stressful, potentially leading to penalties if inaccuracies are discovered.

To avoid such errors, it's crucial to double-check every entry before submitting your tax return. This process might seem tedious, but it's an investment in peace of mind. Consider using tax software with built-in error-checking capabilities. These programs can flag inconsistencies or missing information, guiding you to correct mistakes before finalizing your submission. The use of technology not only streamlines the filing process but also significantly reduces the chance of human error. By leveraging these tools, you can ensure your tax forms reflect an accurate and complete financial picture, protecting you from the hassle of audits and fines.

Staying informed about changes in tax laws is equally important. Tax regulations can shift unexpectedly, and staying updated ensures you remain compliant. Subscribing to updates from the IRS or attending tax seminars can keep you abreast of any new developments. These resources provide valuable insights into the evolving tax landscape, equipping you with the knowledge to adapt your strategies accordingly. Workshops and webinars offer the opportunity to learn directly from experts, clarify complex topics, and answer specific questions you might have. By continually educating yourself, you empower your business to navigate the tax system with confidence and agility.

Let's consider the potential consequences of common tax mistakes. A late payment can result in hefty penalties, eating into your profits and adding financial strain. Similarly, errors in your tax forms can lead to increased scrutiny from tax authorities. An audit consumes time and can damage your reputation, affecting your standing with stakeholders and clients. The stress of undergoing such scrutiny can distract you from running your business, impacting productivity and morale. By avoiding these pitfalls, you preserve your financial health and peace of mind, allowing you to focus on what matters most—growing your business and serving your customers effectively.

5.6 STAYING COMPLIANT: LEGAL CONSIDERATIONS FOR BOOKKEEPERS

Staying compliant with financial regulations is crucial for small businesses, ensuring smooth operations and avoiding legal pitfalls. Compliance requirements often start with meticulous record-keeping, the foundation for all financial activities. Accurate documentation not only aids in financial transparency but also keeps you aligned with regulatory mandates. Maintaining detailed records of transactions, employee wages, and business expenses is not just good practice —it's legally required. Employment tax obligations are another critical area. These taxes, including Social Security, Medicare, and federal unemployment, must be calculated accurately and deposited on time to avoid penalties. Understanding and adhering to these mandates helps ensure your business remains in good standing with tax agencies.

Non-compliance with financial regulations carries significant risks. Failing to meet tax obligations or neglecting proper record-keeping can lead to hefty fines and even legal action. These penalties can be financially crippling, diverting funds away from growth and innovation. Beyond the financial impact, non-compliance can damage your business's reputation. Clients, partners, and investors may question your reliability, leading to a loss of credibility that's hard to rebuild. The damage to your reputation can ripple through your business, affecting relationships and opportunities for years. It's a stark reminder that regulations are not just about following rules but protecting your business's future.

Regular in-house audits and compliance checks are indispensable to maintaining compliance. Think of these as routine health checks for your business. They help identify areas of non-compliance before they become serious issues. Conducting internal audits allows you to review financial practices, ensuring they align with current laws and regulations. Compliance management tools can further streamline this process. These tools help monitor regulatory changes, automate compliance tasks, and provide alerts when potential violations occur. By leveraging technology, you can reduce the burden of manual compliance tasks and stay ahead of regulatory updates, ensuring your business operates smoothly.

Access to reliable compliance resources is vital for staying informed and compliant. Government websites, such as the IRS's Small Business and Self-Employed Tax Center, offer a wealth of information on tax obligations and updates. These resources provide guidance on everything from record-keeping requirements to employment tax obligations, acting as a reliable reference for business owners. Additionally, professional compliance consultations can offer personalized insights into your compliance status. Engaging with a compliance expert ensures you're not just meeting the minimum requirements but optimizing your practices for efficiency and effectiveness. By tapping into these resources, you empower your business with the knowledge and tools needed to thrive in a regulated environment.

In this chapter, we've delved into the nuances of taxation and compliance, covering the gamut from tax obligations to legal considerations. By understanding and implementing these practices, you safeguard your business against potential pitfalls and position it for sustained success. As we transition into the next chapter, we'll explore how to leverage financial insights for strategic decision-making, drawing on the solid foundation of compliance you've established.

6

ENHANCING YOUR BOOKKEEPING EFFICIENCY

Envision your business operating like a finely tuned machine, with every component working seamlessly to maintain smooth operations. Efficient bookkeeping is the lubricant that keeps this machine running without a hitch. For many entrepreneurs, the challenge lies in finding the time to manage their books amidst the hustle and bustle of daily tasks. This chapter aims to arm you with strategies that streamline your financial management, allowing you to focus on what truly matters—growing your business.

6.1 TIME-SAVING BOOKKEEPING TECHNIQUES FOR BUSY ENTREPRENEURS

Consider the art of batching as your new secret weapon against inefficiency. By grouping similar tasks, you create a focused environment that minimizes distractions and maximizes productivity. Think of it like baking a batch of cookies rather than one at a time; it's all about efficiency. Instead of scattering your invoice processing throughout the week, designate a specific day and time to tackle this task in one go. This method sharpens your focus and reduces the mental fatigue of constant task-switching. Similarly, consolidating expense entries into a single session each week allows you to maintain a clear and organized financial picture without the hassle of daily interruptions.

Prioritizing tasks can transform your approach to bookkeeping. Focusing on high-impact activities ensures that your time and energy are spent where they matter most. Begin by identifying tasks that directly affect your cash flow, such as invoicing and bill payments. These should take precedence, as they have immediate financial implications. Setting monthly goals for your bookkeeping tasks can also provide structure and motivation. Whether clearing outstanding invoices or reconciling accounts, having clear targets helps maintain momentum and ensures that nothing falls through the cracks. This strategic approach boosts productivity and enhances your overall financial health.

Delegation is another powerful tool in your efficiency arsenal. Your time is valuable as an entrepreneur, and not every task requires your personal touch. Consider outsourcing tax preparation to a professional who can easily navigate the complexities of tax laws, freeing you to focus on strategic decision-making. Hiring a virtual assistant for data entry tasks can also alleviate your workload while maintaining accuracy. This approach lets you concentrate on your strengths and leverage others' expertise, ultimately benefiting your business. Embracing delegation creates a more balanced workload, enhancing productivity and reducing stress.

Technology can be a game-changer when it comes to saving time in bookkeeping. Various tools are designed to automate or simplify time-consuming tasks, allowing you to work smarter, not harder. Expense-tracking apps with receipt scanning capabilities eliminate manual data entry, ensuring your records are accurate and up-to-date. Software that generates automatic financial reports provides insights at a glance, enabling you to make informed decisions quickly. These tools are like having a personal assistant dedicated to keeping your financial house in order. Integrating them into your routine enhances efficiency and frees time for other essential business activities.

Interactive Element: Time Management Checklist

To help streamline your bookkeeping tasks, consider using this checklist:

- **Batch Similar Tasks:** Allocate specific days for invoicing and expense entries.
- **Prioritize High-Impact Activities:** Focus on tasks that affect cash flow and set monthly goals.
- **Delegate Efficiently:** Outsource complex tasks like tax preparation and hire assistance for data entry.
- **Leverage Technology:** Utilize apps and software that automate tracking and reporting.

This checklist serves as a practical guide to enhance your bookkeeping efficiency, allowing you to focus on strategic growth and business development.

6.2 AUTOMATING BOOKKEEPING TASKS: WHAT YOU NEED TO KNOW

Automation in bookkeeping is like having an assistant who never tires, ensuring that your financial records are accurate and up-to-date without constant supervision. The beauty of automation lies in its ability to reduce human error and save precious time. By streamlining transaction categorization, automation ensures that each entry is correctly classified, minimizing the risk of mistakes. Imagine the ease of having your transactions automatically sorted into revenue, expenses, and other categories. Automation also simplifies recurring billing, so those monthly invoices and payments happen without you lifting a finger. This consistency leads to a smoother cash flow and fewer headaches when reconciling accounts.

Identifying which tasks can be automated is crucial. Bank reconciliation is one area where automation shines. Instead of manually matching transactions with bank statements, automated systems can handle this task swiftly, highlighting any discrepancies for review.

Payroll management also benefits tremendously from automation. It ensures that employee payments are timely and accurate, reducing stress and errors. By automating these functions, you can focus on strategic activities that require your expertise, leaving the routine tasks to technology.

However, implementing automation is not without its challenges. The initial setup can be complex, requiring time and patience to integrate new systems with your existing processes. It's akin to setting up a new piece of equipment; there's a learning curve. Once in place, automation demands regular system updates to keep everything running smoothly. These updates ensure compatibility with new software versions and maintain security, but they can be frustrating if not managed correctly. Understanding these challenges helps anticipate and mitigate potential issues, ensuring a seamless transition to automated bookkeeping.

When selecting automation tools, consider their ease of use and integration capabilities. Tools should simplify processes and fit seamlessly into your current workflow. Evaluating user-friendly interfaces and intuitive design is crucial. You don't want to spend hours deciphering how to use a new tool. Integration with existing software is equally important. Connecting with your other business systems, like inventory or CRM software, enhances efficiency and accuracy. Furthermore, comprehensive customer support can be a lifeline during the transition. Access to knowledgeable support staff and detailed resources can make all the difference in overcoming hurdles and ensuring successful automation implementation.

Tools like Intuit QuickBooks Online are highly recommended for those seeking ideal automation solutions. It is praised for its customizable features and excellent user experience, making it a top choice for small businesses seeking reliable automation [SOURCE 1]. FreshBooks is another option worth considering, especially for service-based businesses. With its intuitive interface and features like time tracking, it simplifies bookkeeping without overwhelming the user. By choosing the right tools, you can transform your bookkeeping from a time-consuming task to an efficient and streamlined process, freeing you to concentrate on growing your business and achieving your goals.

6.3 UTILIZING TEMPLATES TO STAY ORGANIZED

Imagine stepping into a kitchen with a recipe card ready to bake a cake. The recipe provides clear instructions and measurements, ensuring the result is delicious and consistent. In the world of bookkeeping, templates serve a similar purpose. They standardize processes, bringing uniformity and efficiency to your financial management. Consider invoice templates, for instance. They ensure a professional appearance and guarantee that essential information, such as payment terms and contact details, is always included. This consistency helps avoid miscommunication with clients and reduces the chances of payment delays.

Visual Element: Sample Templates

Consider using these examples as a starting point for your templates and checklists:

- **Invoice Template:** Includes fields for client details, itemized services, payment terms, and contact information.

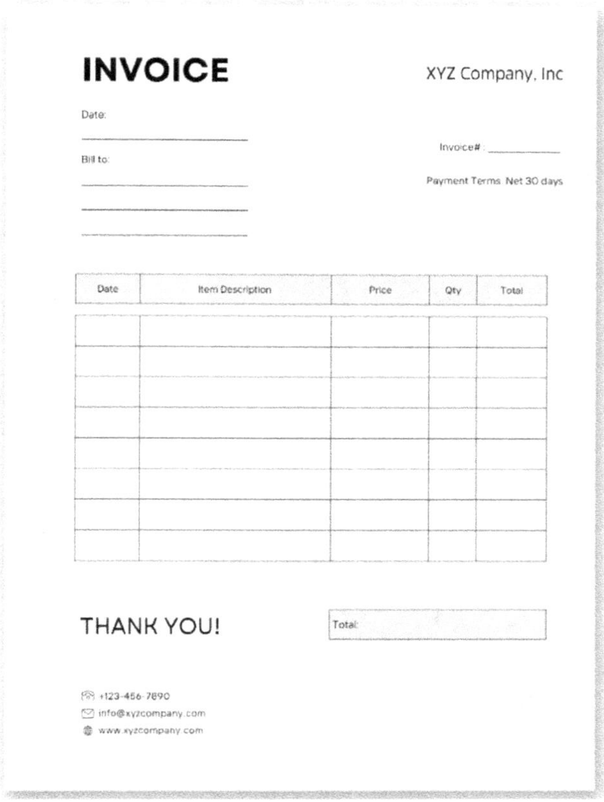

INVOICE

XYZ Company, Inc

Date:

Bill to:

Invoice# : ____________

Payment Terms Net 30 days

Date	Item Description	Price	Qty	Total

THANK YOU!

Total:

+123-456-7890
info@xyzcompany.com
www.xyzcompany.com

- **Quote/Estimate Template:** Details work to be done, terms & conditions and client information.

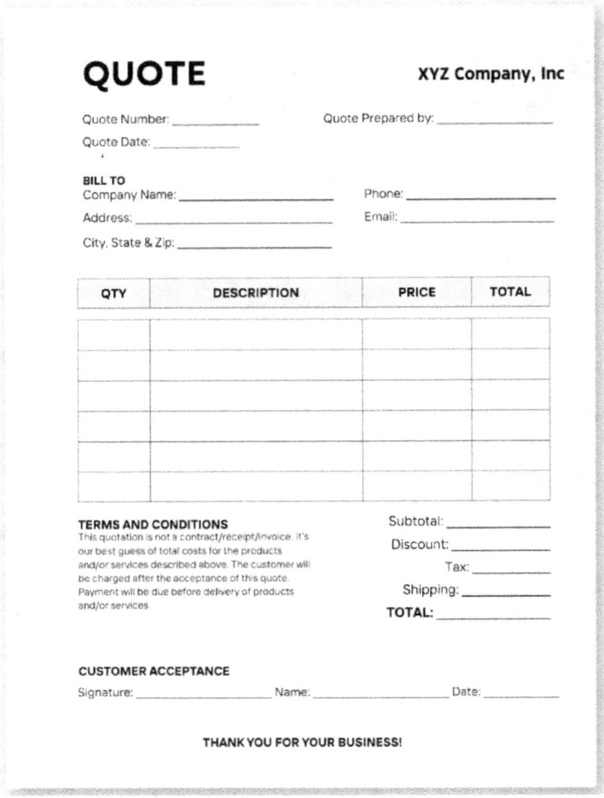

QUOTE

XYZ Company, Inc

Quote Number: ____________ Quote Prepared by: ____________

Quote Date: ____________

BILL TO

Company Name: ____________ Phone: ____________

Address: ____________ Email: ____________

City, State & Zip: ____________

QTY	DESCRIPTION	PRICE	TOTAL

TERMS AND CONDITIONS

This quotation is not a contract/receipt/invoice. It's our best guess of total costs for the products and/or services described above. The customer will be charged after the acceptance of this quote. Payment will be due before delivery of products and/or services

Subtotal: ____________

Discount: ____________

Tax: ____________

Shipping: ____________

TOTAL: ____________

CUSTOMER ACCEPTANCE

Signature: ____________ Name: ____________ Date: ____________

THANK YOU FOR YOUR BUSINESS!

These tools enhance your efficiency and bring a sense of control and order to your financial tasks. By leveraging templates, you build an organizational foundation that supports accurate and timely bookkeeping, allowing you to focus on the bigger picture of your business growth.

6.4 LEVERAGING CLOUD SOLUTIONS FOR FLEXIBILITY

Imagine managing your business finances from any location, whether at home, in a café, or even abroad. This flexibility is one of the key advantages of cloud-based bookkeeping. You gain access from multiple devices by storing your financial data in the cloud, ensuring you're always connected to your accounts. Whether you prefer working from a desktop, tablet, or smartphone, cloud solutions provide the freedom to choose, adapting to your lifestyle and work habits. This accessibility means you can make informed financial decisions in real-time, no matter where you are. Furthermore, cloud-based systems facilitate seamless collaboration with your team. Multiple users can access and update the system simultaneously, ensuring everyone is on the same page. This real-time collaboration enhances efficiency, reduces the risk of errors, and fosters a more cohesive team environment.

Transitioning your bookkeeping operations to the cloud might seem daunting, but it can be a smooth process with the right approach. Start by selecting a cloud provider that aligns with your business's needs. Consider factors like ease of use, integration capabilities, and customer support. Platforms like Intuit QuickBooks Online and Xero are popular choices, known for their user-friendly interfaces and robust features [SOURCE 1]. Once you've chosen a provider, focus on migrating your data securely and efficiently. Be sure to backup your existing data before starting the migration to prevent any loss. Then, follow the provider's guidelines for data transfer, ensuring that all information is accurately imported into the new system. This step is crucial for maintaining data integrity and avoiding discrepancies affecting your financial records.

Security is a top concern when moving to the cloud, and for good reason. Your financial data is sensitive, and protecting it should be a priority. Implementing two-factor authentication is a simple yet effective way to enhance security. This extra layer of protection requires users to verify their identity through a secondary method, such as a text message or authentication app, before accessing the system. Regularly updating access permissions is another critical practice. Review who has access to your financial data and adjust permissions as needed to ensure that only authorized individuals can view or edit sensitive information. By taking these precautions, you safeguard your data against unauthorized access and potential breaches.

The benefits of cloud solutions extend beyond flexibility and security. They also enhance business operations in various ways. One significant advantage is the capability for remote work. With cloud-based systems, you and your team can work from anywhere, promoting a healthy work-life balance and increasing productivity. Additionally, cloud platforms offer automatic software updates and backups. This means you'll always have the latest features and security enhancements without the hassle of manual updates. Automatic backups ensure your data is safe and recoverable during a technical issue or disaster. This peace of mind lets you focus on your business, knowing your financial records are protected and up-to-date.

Cloud solutions are transforming the way businesses manage their finances. Accessing your accounts from any device, collaborating seamlessly with your team, and ensuring data security are just some advantages. By transitioning to the cloud, you enhance your business's flexibility, scalability, and efficiency, allowing you to quickly adapt to changing needs and seize new opportunities. Whether working from home, in a shared office space, or while traveling, cloud-based bookkeeping solutions offer the tools you need to keep your financial operations running smoothly and effectively.

6.5 EVALUATING THE EFFECTIVENESS OF YOUR BOOKKEEPING SYSTEM

Regularly evaluating your bookkeeping system is crucial to ensure it operates efficiently and effectively. These assessments act like routine check-ups for your business's financial health, identifying potential bottlenecks that could slow down processes or lead to inaccuracies. For instance, certain tasks take longer than expected, signaling a need for streamlined procedures or additional resources. Evaluations also ensure compliance with updated regulations, which can change over time and catch you off guard if not monitored. Staying on top of these changes protects your business from penalties and helps maintain a solid reputation. By regularly assessing your system, you can address issues before they become problematic, ensuring smooth operations and peace of mind.

To measure the success of your bookkeeping efforts, you can use specific metrics that provide a clear picture of how well your system is functioning. The accuracy of financial reports is a critical indicator; these reports should reflect the actual financial state of your business without discrepancies. Timeliness is another key metric to consider. How quickly are data entries and reconciliations completed? Delays in these areas can lead to outdated information, affecting decision-making and overall financial strategy. Tracking these performance indicators provides valuable insights into your bookkeeping processes' strengths and areas for improvement. This understanding allows you to make informed adjustments, improving the overall efficiency of your financial management.

Recognizing the signs of an ineffective bookkeeping system is vital for timely intervention. Frequent discrepancies in financial statements are a red flag, indicating potential errors in data entry or categorization. Such inconsistencies can distort your understanding of the business's financial performance, leading to misguided decisions. Additionally, an overwhelming backlog of tasks suggests that your current processes may be inadequate to handle the workload. This backlog can cause stress and burnout, reducing productivity and increasing the likelihood of mistakes. By identifying these symptoms early, you can take action to rectify the situation, ensuring that your bookkeeping remains a reliable backbone for your business.

Improving the efficiency of your bookkeeping system often involves implementing strategic changes. Automation of repetitive tasks is one approach that can yield significant benefits, reducing the time spent on mundane activities and minimizing human error. This shift allows you to allocate resources more effectively, focusing on areas that require critical thinking and analysis. Regular training sessions for bookkeeping staff are another effective strategy. These sessions keep your team updated on the latest tools, techniques, and regulations, ensuring they are well-equipped to handle any challenges. Investing in your team's development enhances their skills and confidence, leading to more accurate and efficient bookkeeping practices.

Visual Element: Performance Evaluation Checklist

To assist with your evaluations, consider using this checklist:

- **Identify Bottlenecks:** Review tasks to pinpoint areas causing delays or inefficiencies.
- **Ensure Compliance:** Verify that your system adheres to current regulations and industry standards.
- **Monitor Accuracy:** Regularly check financial reports for discrepancies and correct them as needed.
- **Assess Timeliness:** Evaluate the speed of data entry and reconciliation processes.
- **Address Backlogs:** Identify and resolve any accumulation of unfinished tasks.
- **Implement Automation:** Use technology to streamline repetitive tasks and reduce errors.
- **Conduct Training:** Schedule regular sessions to keep staff informed and skilled.

By following this checklist, you maintain a proactive approach to managing your bookkeeping system, ensuring it remains a valuable asset in supporting your business's success.

6.6 ADAPTING YOUR BOOKKEEPING PRACTICES AS YOUR BUSINESS GROWS

As your business evolves, so too must your bookkeeping practices. Growth brings complexity, and what once worked for a small operation may no longer suffice. Imagine starting with a simple ledger for a handful of transactions, but as your business expands, the volume of data can quickly become overwhelming. This is where scalable bookkeeping practices come into play, allowing your financial processes to grow alongside your business. Transitioning from manual to automated systems can be a game-changer, offering the ability to handle increased transactions with precision and efficiency. Similarly, expanding your chart of accounts becomes necessary as your operations diversify, ensuring that every aspect of your business's financial activity is accurately captured and categorized. This adaptability is crucial for maintaining clarity and control in a dynamic business environment.

Identifying the right moment to adapt your bookkeeping practices is key to effectively managing growth. Look for specific business developments that signal a need for change. An increased volume of transactions is a clear indicator that your current system may need an upgrade. As sales grow, manual entry becomes untenable, and automation can offer a solution, streamlining operations and reducing errors. Introducing new revenue streams—such as launching a new product line or service—also necessitates changes in your bookkeeping. These developments require adjustments to your financial tracking to ensure accurate reporting and analysis. Recognizing these triggers early allows for proactive adjustments, preventing your bookkeeping from becoming a bottleneck in your business growth.

To manage growth effectively, consider strategies that scale your bookkeeping systems to accommodate expansion. Upgrading to comprehensive accounting software can provide the tools to handle increased complexity. These systems often offer features tailored to diverse business needs, including advanced reporting, real-time analytics, and integration with other business applications. Investing in such software ensures that your bookkeeping can meet your business's demands. Additionally, hiring additional bookkeeping staff may become necessary as your business grows. This investment in human resources spreads the workload and brings expertise that can enhance accuracy and efficiency. Collaborating with skilled professionals allows you to focus on strategic growth while ensuring that your financial records remain reliable and insightful.

Consider the example of a startup that began with a straightforward bookkeeping system but soon found it inadequate as its customer base expanded. They could automate routine tasks by transitioning to a more robust system, freeing time for strategic analysis and planning. This shift allowed them to scale operations without sacrificing accuracy or control. Similarly, a small business integrating new technology to handle an increased workload illustrates the importance of adaptability. By adopting innovative solutions, they managed to streamline their processes, improve efficiency, and maintain a high level of customer service, even as their demands grew. These examples highlight the importance of evolving bookkeeping practices to support your business's success.

Adapting your bookkeeping practices is ongoing, requiring constant evaluation and adjustment. By understanding the need for scalable systems, recognizing triggers for change, and implementing effective strategies, you ensure that your bookkeeping remains a powerful tool in your business arsenal. As we transition into the next chapter, we'll explore how leveraging your bookkeeping insights can drive strategic decisions and foster sustainable growth.

7

LEVERAGING BOOKKEEPING FOR STRATEGIC DECISIONS

Picture yourself standing on a hilltop overlooking a vast landscape where every detail symbolizes a different facet of your business. This vantage point allows you to see potential paths and obstacles, much like strategic planning relies on a clear view of your financial data. Accurate bookkeeping transforms your ledgers into a powerful map, guiding you to set realistic financial targets and allocate resources precisely. By understanding your data, you make informed choices that align with your business's long-term goals, avoiding pitfalls and seizing opportunities that propel you forward.

7.1 USING FINANCIAL DATA FOR BUSINESS PLANNING

Strategic planning thrives on the integrity of your financial data. It's this data that provides the foundation for setting achievable financial targets. Imagine you're a ship captain navigating the seas; your journey is uncertain without a compass. In business, financial data serves as your compass, pointing you toward objectives that are not only ambitious but also attainable. By analyzing past performance, you set benchmarks reflecting your business's potential. This clarity allows you to allocate resources efficiently, ensuring that every dollar spent moves you closer to your goals. Whether investing in new technology or expanding your workforce, data-driven decisions ensure that resources are used wisely and effectively.

Integrating financial data into your business plans involves more than just number crunching. It requires aligning your financial metrics with strategic goals and creating a cohesive vision that guides decision-making. Funded by historical data, budget forecasts become potent tools for predicting future trends. This foresight allows you to anticipate changes in the market and adjust your strategies accordingly. By linking these forecasts to your objectives, you create a roadmap that charts a course for success, enabling you to navigate challenges confidently and quickly. This process transforms raw numbers into actionable insights, ensuring your business plans are grounded in reality.

The importance of data-driven decision-making cannot be overemphasized. In an era where relying solely on instincts can lead to missed opportunities, combining intuition with data analysis enhances outcomes significantly. Accurate financial information reduces risk and uncertainty, providing a solid foundation for making decisions that affect your business's future. It also improves accountability and transparency, as data-based decisions are easier to justify and evaluate. This approach fosters a culture of informed decision-making, where every choice is scrutinized and supported by evidence, leading to improved strategic outcomes and stronger financial health.

Consider the real-world examples of businesses that have harnessed financial data to achieve remarkable success. A startup, for instance, used cash flow projections to plan its expansion, ensuring it had the liquidity to support new ventures without compromising existing operations. By analyzing cash flow trends, the company identified times of surplus and shortage, allowing it to time investments strategically. Similarly, a retail business adjusted its inventory based on sales data, optimizing stock levels to meet customer demand while minimizing excess. This data-driven approach reduced carrying costs and improved cash flow, demonstrating the power of financial data in driving operational efficiency and growth.

Interactive Element: Financial Data Integration Exercise

To apply these concepts, take a moment to review your financial data. Identify trends and patterns that could inform your strategic planning. Are there areas where resources could be reallocated for better results? Consider how your budget forecasts align with your business goals. Use this information to adjust your plans, ensuring they reflect the realities of your financial landscape. This exercise reinforces the importance of integrating financial data into your business strategy, empowering you to make informed decisions that drive success.

The strategic use of financial data transforms how you approach business planning. It empowers you to set realistic targets, allocate resources wisely, and navigate challenges with foresight. Integrating financial metrics into your plans creates a cohesive vision that guides your business toward its goals. With accurate data at your fingertips, you can make informed decisions that enhance your business's performance and potential.

7.2 IDENTIFYING TRENDS AND PATTERNS IN YOUR FINANCIALS

Spotting trends in your financial data is like finding a hidden pattern in a complex tapestry. You begin by compiling your financial records over time, focusing on key metrics such as revenue, expenses, and cash flow. This historical data acts as a lens, allowing you to zoom in on specific areas that can reveal much about your business's performance. Trend analysis involves comparing these metrics across different monthly, quarterly, or annual periods to see how your business is evolving. Are sales rising steadily, or do they fluctuate with the seasons? Are operating costs creeping up, eroding your profit margins? By identifying these patterns, you gain valuable insights into the forces shaping your business, helping you anticipate challenges and seize new opportunities.

Visualizing these trends through charts and graphs can transform abstract numbers into concrete insights. For example, a line graph showing monthly sales can highlight seasonal peaks and troughs, helping you prepare for demand surges or slumps. A bar chart comparing quarterly expenses can reveal areas where costs consistently rise, prompting you to investigate further. These visual tools simplify complex data, making it easier to communicate findings to stakeholders or team members. They provide a snapshot of your business's performance, clearly showing where you're thriving and where adjustments are needed. By regularly updating these visualizations, you keep a finger on the pulse of your business, ready to pivot strategies as needed.

Recognizing patterns in your financials is crucial for identifying both opportunities and threats. Seasonal sales fluctuations, for example, might suggest timing promotions or inventory orders to capitalize on peak demand. If you notice consistent increases in operating costs, it may indicate inefficiencies that must be addressed. These patterns tell a story, guiding you to make informed decisions that align with your business's goals. By understanding the underlying causes of these patterns, you can implement strategies that enhance profitability and sustainability. This proactive approach lets you stay ahead of challenges, ensuring your business remains competitive and resilient in a changing market.

The right tools and methodologies can enhance your ability to conduct trend analysis effectively. Excel is a powerful tool for data visualization, offering a range of charts and graphs that simplify the analysis process. By inputting your financial data into Excel, you can create dynamic visualizations that update automatically, providing real-time insights. Business intelligence tools take this further, offering advanced features like predictive analytics and detailed reporting. These tools can uncover hidden patterns, helping you confidently make data-driven decisions. By investing time in learning these technologies, you equip yourself with the skills to navigate your financial landscape precisely.

Consider a case study where trend analysis led to strategic advantages. A company noticed a sharp increase in sales during the holiday season, prompting it to ramp up marketing efforts and stock levels in anticipation. As a result, it maximized revenue during peak periods, outperforming competitors who didn't adjust their strategies. In another example, a business observed shifts in consumer behavior patterns through data analysis, leading to a successful marketing campaign tailored to changing preferences. By aligning its strategies with these insights, the company achieved higher engagement and conversion rates, demonstrating the power of trend analysis in driving business success.

7.3 MAKING INFORMED BUSINESS DECISIONS WITH BOOKKEEPING INSIGHTS

Imagine a ship navigating through foggy waters. Decisions are based on guesswork rather than certainty without clear visibility, which can lead to disaster. Making decisions without insights from your financial data can be just as treacherous in business. The information embedded within your bookkeeping records is like the beacon that guides you, clarifying the complexities you face. By leveraging these insights, you can enhance your business's success, ensuring that each financial move is rooted in reality rather than speculation. One of the profound impacts of informed decision-making is increased profitability through effective cost control. By analyzing expenses and identifying areas where costs can be reduced or optimized, you create room for more significant profit margins. This approach involves regular monitoring of expenses and comparing them against industry standards to pinpoint inefficiencies. It's about understanding the story your numbers tell and using this narrative to streamline operations, reduce waste, and allocate resources more effectively. With clear insights, you can also spot opportunities for investment in growth. Whether expanding your product line, entering new markets, or upgrading technology, informed decisions allow you to weigh risks and rewards precisely. The data is your compass, ensuring growth initiatives align with financial health and strategic goals.

You need a systematic approach to extract actionable insights from your financial data. Start by comparing financial ratios over time. These ratios, such as return on investment (ROI) or current ratio, provide a snapshot of your business's financial health and performance. By tracking these metrics, you can identify trends, strengths, and areas for improvement. Evaluating profit margins against industry benchmarks is another critical step. This comparison helps you understand how your business stacks up against competitors, offering insights into areas where you might gain a competitive edge. By understanding where you stand, you can tailor strategies that capitalize on strengths and address weaknesses. This methodical analysis turns data into a powerful tool, guiding strategic decisions that propel your business forward.

The benefits of data-driven decisions are exemplified by businesses that have successfully leveraged insights for strategic advantage. Consider a company that optimized its supply chain operations by analyzing inventory turnover and supplier performance data. This insight allowed the company to reduce excess stock, negotiate better terms with suppliers, and improve delivery times, resulting in significant cost savings and enhanced customer satisfaction. In another instance, a business decided to expand its product line after a thorough analysis revealed a growing demand for complementary products. The company captured new revenue streams by aligning product development with market trends and customer preferences and solidified its market position. These examples highlight the transformative power of data to inform decisions, demonstrating how insights can lead to strategic breakthroughs and sustained success.

Ignoring data insights can lead to potential pitfalls that undermine business success. Relying on assumptions rather than evidence often results in missed opportunities for cost savings. Without a clear understanding of where your money is going, you risk overspending in areas that offer little return. This oversight can erode profit margins and limit resources available for strategic initiatives. Additionally, unanticipated financial downturns can catch businesses off guard, especially when decisions are made without considering the full scope of financial data. The failure to anticipate these downturns can lead to cash flow issues, operational disruptions, and even jeopardize the business's survival. By ignoring the insights data provides, you gamble with your business's future, leaving it vulnerable to risks that could have been mitigated with informed decision-making.

Informed decision-making is not just a strategic advantage; it's necessary in today's competitive business landscape. By embracing the insights from your bookkeeping, you empower yourself to navigate challenges confidently and precisely. This proactive approach ensures that your business remains agile, resilient, and poised for growth, no matter what the future holds.

7.4 THE IMPORTANCE OF REGULAR FINANCIAL REVIEWS

Imagine trying to keep a car running smoothly without ever checking the oil or the tire pressure. Just as regular maintenance prevents breakdowns, periodic financial reviews are vital to maintaining your business's financial health. These reviews allow you to spot discrepancies early, like catching a leak before it becomes a flood. By systematically assessing your financial records, you ensure that no error goes unnoticed, whether it's a misclassified expense or an overlooked payment. This proactive approach helps you maintain accuracy and transparency, laying a strong foundation for sustainable growth.

Tracking progress toward financial goals is another crucial aspect of regular reviews. Think of these goals as milestones on a road map. Without regular check-ins, you might find yourself veering off course. By evaluating your progress quarterly, you can measure how well your business performs against its objectives. Are you hitting your revenue targets? Are expenses creeping up faster than anticipated? These insights guide you in making adjustments and keeping your business on track toward achieving its ambitions. This continuous evaluation helps you allocate resources effectively, ensuring that efforts are aligned with strategic priorities.

Conducting effective financial reviews requires a structured framework. Start with quarterly performance evaluations that dive deep into your financial statements. These evaluations provide a snapshot of your business's health, highlighting strengths and areas needing improvement. Use key performance indicators (KPIs) to measure success, focusing on metrics that reflect your business's core activities. Are your profit margins healthy? Is cash flow steady? Regularly assessing these indicators clarifies your business's performance, helping you make informed decisions. This systematic approach transforms reviews from a routine task into a powerful tool for strategic oversight.

Financial reviews are pivotal in strategic adjustment, acting as a compass for necessary course corrections. When financial outcomes deviate from expectations, reviews prompt a reevaluation of resources. Perhaps a marketing campaign isn't delivering the expected return, or a new product line is underperforming. You ensure that investments yield the best results by reallocating resources based on review outcomes. Additionally, reviews help you adjust business strategies in response to market changes. If demand for a product shifts or a new competitor enters the field, timely reviews allow you to pivot strategies, capitalizing on opportunities and mitigating risks.

Consider businesses that have thrived by adopting regular review practices. One company refined its pricing strategy after a review revealed that its products were priced too low compared to competitors. By adjusting prices, it increased revenue without sacrificing sales volume. Another organization improved operational efficiency by identifying bottlenecks in its supply chain during a review. Streamlining processes and renegotiating supplier contracts reduced costs and improved delivery times. These examples demonstrate how regular reviews drive success, offering actionable insights that refine strategies and enhance performance.

Textual Element: Review Process Checklist

To implement effective financial reviews, consider the following steps:

- Schedule quarterly reviews to evaluate financial statements and KPIs.
- Compare actual performance against financial goals, noting deviations.
- Identify areas for resource reallocation based on review outcomes.
- Adjust business strategies in response to market changes and review insights.
- Document findings and action plans to guide future decision-making.

This checklist serves as a practical guide, ensuring that your financial reviews are thorough and strategic. It empowers you to confidently navigate your business landscape, ready to seize opportunities and address challenges as they arise. Regular financial reviews are about keeping your books in order and steering your business toward a successful and sustainable future.

7.5 BUILDING A FINANCIAL STRATEGY BASED ON YOUR BOOKKEEPING

Crafting a financial strategy is akin to building a sturdy bridge that connects where your business stands today to where you envision it in the future. This strategy is integral to your overall business plan, ensuring that your financial goals align seamlessly with your broader vision. It's about prioritizing long-term sustainability over short-term gains, establishing a path that's not just about growth but sustainable growth. To create a robust financial strategy, begin by setting clear financial objectives. These objectives should reflect your current capabilities and aspirations, serving as the guiding stars that keep your business on course. Defining these objectives requires a deep understanding of your business's strengths and weaknesses and the market landscape in which you operate. Once your objectives are clear, identify the key financial drivers that will propel you toward these goals. These drivers could include factors like sales growth, expense management, or investment in innovation. Recognizing these elements helps you focus on what truly matters, ensuring that every decision contributes to your strategic aims.

Bookkeeping is crucial in strategy development, acting as the foundation for your financial plans. Accurate records provide the historical data needed to set realistic targets, offering a window into past performance and helping predict future trends. This information is invaluable for scenario planning, enabling you to map out potential financial challenges and devise strategies to overcome them. Imagine you're an explorer charting a new territory; the maps you create from your historical data guide you through uncharted territory, helping you navigate obstacles and seize opportunities. By grounding your strategy in solid data, you reduce uncertainty and enhance your ability to make informed decisions that drive success.

Consider the practical applications of strategic financial planning. One effective approach is diversifying revenue streams, which can stabilize your income and reduce dependency on a single source. For instance, a business might expand its product line or explore new markets, spreading risk and opening new avenues for growth. This diversification ensures that your business remains resilient, even in the face of market fluctuations. Another strategic move is implementing cost-reduction initiatives, which can enhance profitability by streamlining operations and eliminating waste. This might involve renegotiating supplier contracts, optimizing production processes, or investing in technology that boosts efficiency. You create a balanced strategy supporting long-term sustainability and success by focusing on revenue growth and cost control.

The beauty of a well-crafted financial strategy lies in its ability to transform potential challenges into opportunities. It equips you with the tools to anticipate changes in the market, adapt to new trends, and innovate in ways that keep your business competitive. This strategic foresight allows you to stay ahead of the curve, positioning your business to survive and thrive in an ever-evolving landscape. As you refine your strategy, remember that it is not a static document but a living framework that evolves with your business. Regularly review and adjust your plans to reflect changing circumstances, ensuring your strategy remains relevant and effective.

In this chapter, we've explored how leveraging bookkeeping can drive strategic decisions, turning financial data into a powerful tool for growth and sustainability. As you refine and implement these strategies, remember that the financial landscape is dynamic, requiring ongoing attention and adaptation. In the next chapter, we'll delve into practical applications and case studies that illustrate these principles in action, providing real-world examples and insights to guide your strategic journey.

8

REAL-LIFE APPLICATIONS AND CASE STUDIES

Picture a bustling retail store on a Saturday afternoon, aisles filled with eager shoppers, cash registers constantly ringing, and employees hustling to keep pace. This vibrant scene showcases the daily challenges retail businesses face, where managing inventory and tracking sales are not just tasks but essential elements that dictate a store's success. Retailers, especially small ones, grapple with high volumes of daily transactions that require meticulous attention to detail. Each sale, refund, and exchange has to be recorded accurately. Imagine the chaos if just one day's worth of sales went unrecorded. Seasonal fluctuations add another layer of complexity. During the holidays, sales might surge dramatically, while during other periods, they might slow to a trickle. Balancing this ebb and flow is crucial to maintaining a healthy bottom line.

8.1 CASE STUDY: BOOKKEEPING FOR A RETAIL BUSINESS

Inventory management is the lifeline of any retail business. It involves more than just counting products on shelves; it requires a strategic approach to ensure stock levels align with customer demand. Accurate inventory records are crucial for financial health. They help prevent overstocking, which ties up capital unnecessarily, and understocking, which risks missed sales opportunities. Consider the task of inventory count reconciliation—it's like taking a snapshot of your store's stock at a given moment. This process helps verify that what you have on paper matches what's physically present, a vital check that keeps financial records in sync with reality. Tracking the cost of goods sold (COGS) is another critical aspect. COGS represents the direct costs associated with producing the goods your business sells, and accurately tracking this figure is essential for calculating profitability. By understanding the relationship between your inventory and COGS, you can better manage your pricing strategies and profit margins.

Point-of-sale (POS) systems are pivotal in streamlining transaction recording and inventory management. Modern POS systems do more than process sales; they integrate with accounting software to automate data entry, reducing the risk of human error. Imagine scanning a product at checkout, and instantly, the sale is recorded, inventory is adjusted, and the financial records are updated in real-time. This seamless integration lets you focus on customer service instead of getting bogged down in administrative tasks. Real-time sales tracking offers invaluable insights into buying patterns, helping you make informed decisions about restocking and promotions. By having a clear view of what's selling and what's not, you can adapt swiftly to consumer demands and optimize your inventory.

Managing accounts payable and receivable effectively is crucial for maintaining cash flow in a retail environment. Vendor payment scheduling is one strategy that helps ensure bills are paid on time without straining cash reserves. By negotiating favorable payment terms with suppliers, you can balance the timing of outflows with your expected inflows. On the other hand, customer credit management is equally important. Offering credit terms to customers can boost sales, but it requires careful monitoring to ensure timely repayments. Implementing a system to track accounts receivable helps maintain a steady cash flow and reduces the risk of defaults. By staying on top of payables and receivables, you can navigate the financial complexities of retail with greater ease and confidence.

Interactive Element: Inventory Management Checklist

To help you manage your retail inventory effectively, consider using this checklist:

- **Conduct Regular Inventory Counts**: Schedule periodic counts to reconcile physical stock with records.
- **Track Cost of Goods Sold (COGS)**: Monitor COGS to understand profitability and adjust pricing strategies.
- **Utilize POS Integration**: Ensure your POS system syncs with accounting software for real-time updates.
- **Schedule Vendor Payments**: Align payment schedules with cash flow to manage expenses.
- **Monitor Customer Credit**: Implement a system for tracking receivables and ensure timely collections.

By implementing these strategies, you can create a robust foundation for your retail business, ensuring that your financial practices support growth and profitability.

8.2 SCENARIO ANALYSIS: FREELANCERS AND SOLE PROPRIETORS

Imagine waking up each morning as a freelancer or sole proprietor, where your income feels like a rollercoaster ride. One month, you're inundated with projects; the next, your inbox sits eerily empty. Unlike regular salaried workers, you don't have the luxury of a steady paycheck. This variability makes bookkeeping both a challenge and a necessity. You must keep a keen eye on your finances, ensuring every dollar earned and spent is accounted for. Here, project-based income variability is your reality. Each project might pay differently, with varying timelines and payment terms, leaving you juggling cash flow like a circus performer. To navigate this, you need to separate business from personal expenses meticulously. Mixing the two can lead to chaos when tax season arrives. Clear boundaries help create a transparent picture of your business's financial health, enabling you to make informed decisions.

Tax considerations for freelancers add another layer of complexity. As a self-employed individual, you are responsible for managing your taxes. This includes self-employment tax obligations, which cover Social Security and Medicare contributions. Unlike traditional employees, these aren't withheld from your paycheck, so you must plan ahead. Estimated taxes become a quarterly ritual, requiring you to project your annual income and set aside the necessary funds. Failure to do so can result in hefty penalties. Additionally, you may qualify for home office deductions if you use part of your home exclusively for business. This deduction can provide significant tax savings, but it requires diligent record-keeping. It's crucial to differentiate between personal and business use to avoid complications during an audit.

Managing cash flow is essential for freelancers to maintain financial stability. Creating a cash reserve fund is a safety net during lean months, providing a buffer against unforeseen expenses. This reserve allows you to cover essential costs even when income is sparse. Equally important is invoicing promptly and consistently. Delayed invoices can disrupt cash flow, so establishing a routine for billing clients ensures a steady income stream. Consistent follow-ups on overdue payments help maintain positive client relationships and keep your finances in check. By adopting these strategies, you can weather the ups and downs of freelancing with greater ease.

Consider the story of a freelance graphic designer who successfully navigated these challenges. Initially overwhelmed by fluctuating income, she implemented a rigorous system for tracking expenses and separating business from personal finances. She stabilized her cash flow by promptly setting up a cash reserve and invoicing clients. Her meticulous approach to managing self-employment taxes and home office deductions resulted in significant savings. This proactive mindset allowed her to focus on her creative work without worrying about financial instability. Her journey is a testament to the power of effective bookkeeping practices for freelancers.

In the realm of managing client payments, communication is key. Clear terms outlined in contracts can prevent misunderstandings and ensure timely payments. This includes specifying payment terms, late fees, and acceptable payment methods upfront. Regular communication with clients about upcoming invoices and payment schedules maintains transparency and fosters trust. By keeping clients informed and involved, freelancers can reduce disputes and ensure a smoother cash flow. These practices enhance financial stability and strengthen professional relationships, paving the way for long-term success in the freelance world.

8.3 MANAGING FINANCES IN A SERVICE-BASED BUSINESS

When you operate a service-based business, you quickly realize that your financial landscape differs significantly from those dealing in tangible products. In this realm, time and labor costs take center stage. Imagine a consultant juggling multiple projects; tracking billable hours becomes crucial here. Every minute spent with a client directly translates into revenue, making it vital to log these hours meticulously. This principle applies whether you're a graphic designer, a marketing strategist, or a personal trainer. Calculating service rates accurately requires understanding your costs and desired profit margins. You must consider the value of your expertise, the time you invest, and the market rate to ensure your pricing is competitive yet sustainable.

Efficient time management is a linchpin in service-based bookkeeping. Tools like Toggl offer a seamless way to track hours worked, providing a clear record of time spent on each task. This software allows you to categorize activities, making it easier to understand where your time goes and how it translates to income. Besides tracking time, managing expenses effectively ensures profitability.

Implementing structured expense reimbursement processes is crucial. This involves setting clear policies for what qualifies as a reimbursable expense and maintaining detailed records. These processes ensure that costs incurred during service delivery are captured accurately, allowing you to maintain a realistic view of your financial health.

How you handle client invoicing and revenue recognition is pivotal. In a service-based business, timely payment isn't just about maintaining cash flow; it's about sustaining client relationships. Consider milestone-based invoicing, where you bill clients at specific project phases. This method ensures a steady flow of income and keeps clients engaged in the project's progress. Retainer agreements, on the other hand, provide financial stability by securing a set fee for ongoing services. These agreements clarify expectations, allowing both parties to plan effectively. They also have significant financial implications, often requiring upfront payment that can stabilize your cash flow and enable better budgeting.

Real-world examples bring these concepts to life. Take a consulting firm that manages a portfolio of diverse clients. Tracking billable hours ensures that every consultation translates into revenue, while milestone invoicing keeps cash flow predictable. Retainer agreements become indispensable when dealing with recurring service contracts, such as monthly marketing services. They provide a reliable income stream, reducing the anxiety often accompanying fluctuating client demands. These contracts are carefully structured to reflect the scope of work, deliverables, and anticipated outcomes, creating a sense of security for the provider and the client.

Incorporating these strategies into your service-based business ensures that your bookkeeping practices support, rather than hinder, your growth. By focusing on time management and accurate expense tracking, you create a financial ecosystem where revenue is predictable, expenses are controlled, and profitability is achievable. The intricate dance of managing time and costs becomes second nature, allowing you to concentrate on what truly matters: delivering exceptional service to your clients and growing your business with confidence.

8.4 BOOKKEEPING CHALLENGES FOR STARTUPS

Startups are dynamic creatures, often born from a spark of innovation and driven by the desire to disrupt the status quo. Yet, behind the scenes, they face many financial challenges that can make or break their success. One of the primary hurdles is securing initial funding. Whether it's bootstrapping, attracting angel investors, or securing venture capital, each path comes with its own set of bookkeeping demands. These funding strategies require meticulous tracking of incoming and outgoing funds to ensure every penny is accounted for. Developing a robust budgeting process becomes crucial as you chart your startup's course. You'll need to anticipate expenses and align them with projected revenues, which demands precision and foresight. This forward-thinking approach lays the groundwork for successful cash flow forecasting, helping you plan for growth and prepare for unexpected financial hiccups.

Establishing strong financial controls is another cornerstone of sustainable startup growth. Without them, you risk errors and fraud undermining your hard work. Implementing approval processes for expenses ensures that every financial decision is scrutinized, preventing unnecessary or unauthorized spending. It's like having a built-in checkpoint that protects your resources. Equally important is the segregation of duties within financial roles. Assigning distinct responsibilities to different individuals reduces the risk of fraudulent activities and enhances accountability. This division of labor ensures that no single person controls all aspects of financial transactions, creating a system of checks and balances that fortifies your startup's financial integrity.

As your startup gains traction, scaling your bookkeeping efforts becomes imperative. What worked for a team of two may not suffice as your business expands. Transitioning from basic spreadsheets to sophisticated accounting software can streamline processes and improve accuracy. Software solutions offer automation features that reduce manual entry errors and save valuable time. They also provide comprehensive reporting tools that deliver insights into your business's financial performance. As your needs evolve, consider hiring or outsourcing accounting functions. Bringing in experts can alleviate the burden on your team, allowing you to focus on strategic growth initiatives. Outsourcing, in particular, offers flexibility and access to specialized skills, ensuring your financial management keeps pace with your business's ambitions.

Consider the inspiring story of a tech startup that successfully navigated these challenges. Initially, they struggled with cash flow issues and rudimentary bookkeeping practices. They gained a clear view of their financial landscape by implementing robust financial controls and transitioning to an advanced accounting system. This newfound clarity allowed them to forecast cash flow accurately and make informed decisions about scaling their operations. As their business grew, they outsourced complex financial tasks to a team of experts, freeing up internal resources for innovation and development. Lessons from their journey highlight the importance of adaptability and the strategic use of technology in overcoming bookkeeping challenges. Through effective financial management, they transformed potential pitfalls into stepping stones for growth, illustrating that startups can thrive in even the most competitive environments with the right tools and mindset.

8.5 LESSONS FROM COMMON BOOKKEEPING PITFALLS

In the whirlwind of running a business, bookkeeping often sits on the back burner, waiting patiently behind more pressing tasks. Yet, ignoring regular reconciliation can lead to a cascade of financial mismanagement. You might think a missed reconciliation here and there is harmless, but these minor lapses accumulate over time into a significant problem. When bank statements don't match your financial records, you risk overdrawing accounts or overlooking errors that could have been caught early. It's like neglecting to check the oil in your car; eventually, the engine seizes, leaving you stranded. Regular reconciliation is your safeguard, ensuring that your financial health stays robust and discrepancies are caught before they become disasters.

Another frequent pitfall is failing to update financial records consistently. Imagine trying to piece together last month's income and expenses from memory—details blur, and inaccuracies creep in. This inconsistency can warp your financial picture, affecting everything from cash flow forecasts to tax filings. Businesses can spiral into financial chaos without up-to-date records, making it challenging to assess performance accurately or make informed decisions. A structured approach is necessary to prevent these issues, with a set schedule for updating records, ensuring nothing is left to chance. Think of it as setting a regular appointment with your finances that keeps your business running smoothly.

To combat these common errors, establishing a reconciliation schedule is crucial. Determine a frequency that suits your business—weekly, bi-weekly, or monthly—and stick to it. This discipline helps identify discrepancies early before they snowball into insurmountable issues. Implementing checklists for routine tasks is another effective strategy. These checklists act as reminders, ensuring no step is overlooked in the hustle of daily operations. They provide a simple yet powerful way to maintain consistency and accuracy, much like a pilot's pre-flight checklist ensures a safe journey (or, in this case, a financially sound business).

The impact of poor bookkeeping reverberates throughout a business. Inaccurate financial reporting can mislead stakeholders, leading to misguided decisions or lost opportunities. When your financial snapshots are unreliable, strategizing becomes a guessing game rather than a calculated effort. Moreover, missed tax deadlines can invite penalties that drain your hard-earned profits, adding unnecessary stress to tax season. Compliance lapses can tarnish a business's reputation, making securing loans or attracting investors harder. In short, poor bookkeeping doesn't just affect your books—it undermines the entire foundation of your business.

Consider the story of a small retail business that teetered on the edge of collapse due to neglected bookkeeping practices. Once they recognized the severity of their situation, they took decisive action, implementing a reconciliation schedule and revisiting their financial records with a fine-toothed comb. This commitment to accuracy and transparency turned their fortunes around; within months, they were back on track and identifying new growth opportunities. Similarly, a non-profit organization struggled with compliance issues stemming from disorganized records. By overhauling their bookkeeping system and fostering a culture of accountability, they regained donor trust and secured funding for future projects. These stories highlight the transformative power of diligent bookkeeping, showing that even when a business falters, recovery is possible with the right strategies and mindset.

8.6 SUCCESS STORIES: MASTERING BOOKKEEPING BASICS

Imagine a small cafe tucked away on a bustling street, where the scent of freshly brewed coffee mingles with the chatter of satisfied customers. This cafe once struggled with financial chaos—receipts stuffed in drawers, expenses tracked haphazardly, and a general sense of unease whenever numbers were involved. The owner realized that to truly thrive, she needed to get a grip on her finances. She turned to bookkeeping with determination, starting with cost control measures. By diligently tracking every expense and analyzing her supply chain, she discovered areas where she could cut costs without sacrificing quality. This newfound efficiency boosted her profitability, allowing her to reinvest in her business. With clear financial data, she began making decisions based on facts, not guesswork. The cafe soon flourished, expanding its menu and attracting a loyal customer base.

Another inspiring story comes from a tech startup that once teetered on the brink of financial uncertainty. The founders knew their innovative product had potential, but without clear financial insights, they were flying blind. They decided to leverage technology to bring efficiency to their bookkeeping practices. By integrating advanced accounting software, they automated tedious tasks, allowing them to focus on strategic growth. This shift not only improved their data accuracy but also saved countless hours. As they built a culture of financial accountability, their team became more conscious of spending, fostering a sense of shared responsibility. The founders could forecast more effectively with accurate data, securing funding and scaling their operations. Their journey highlights the transformative power of embracing technology and fostering a financially literate environment.

Continuous improvement in bookkeeping is not just beneficial; it's essential. Businesses that thrive understand that standing still is not an option. Regular training and skill-building keep the team sharp and adaptable. One retail company, for instance, invested in quarterly workshops to ensure their staff stayed updated on the latest financial tools and regulations—this commitment to learning paid off. Employees identified inefficiencies and proposed solutions, leading to streamlined processes and enhanced productivity. The company's ability to adapt to changing financial landscapes ensured long-term success. Adapting to market shifts became second nature, enabling them to pivot swiftly and capitalize on new opportunities.

The power of mastering bookkeeping becomes even more apparent through the voices of those who have experienced it firsthand. One entrepreneur shared how gaining financial literacy transformed his business trajectory. By understanding the nuances of his financial statements, he could negotiate better terms with suppliers and secure favorable loans. His confidence grew as he realized the control he had over his business's destiny. Another business owner testified to the peace of mind that came with financial clarity. No longer dreading tax season or unexpected expenses, she could focus on innovation and growth, knowing her financial foundation was solid.

These stories illustrate the practical benefits of effective bookkeeping and its profound impact on a business's culture and mindset. Businesses become more resilient, adaptable, and poised for growth when embracing financial literacy. As we explore further, remember that the principles of sound financial management are within reach for everyone, regardless of background or experience. The next chapter will delve into leveraging these principles for strategic advantage, ensuring you're prepared to navigate the financial aspects of your business with confidence and foresight.

9

EMPOWERMENT THROUGH BOOKKEEPING

Imagine standing before a mountain, its peak shrouded in mist and mystery. This mountain represents the world of bookkeeping, often perceived as daunting and insurmountable, especially for those new to its challenges. But like any mountain, it can be climbed with the right tools and mindset. You might feel overwhelmed or uncertain about where to start, but remember, every expert was once a beginner. Confidence in your bookkeeping abilities is like a compass, guiding you to navigate this terrain with assurance and clarity. It's about understanding your current skills, identifying areas for growth, and celebrating the milestones along your journey. By focusing on self-assessment and continuous improvement, you can transform bookkeeping from a source of anxiety into a platform for empowerment.

9.1 BUILDING CONFIDENCE IN YOUR BOOKKEEPING ABILITIES

The first step in building confidence is self-assessment. Take a moment to evaluate your current skills and knowledge in bookkeeping. This reflection is not about highlighting shortcomings but recognizing where you stand and where you can grow. Create personal benchmarks for skill improvement. Set realistic goals that challenge yet motivate you. For instance, if reconciling accounts feels overwhelming, break it down into smaller tasks. Reflect on past successes and challenges, recognizing patterns that can guide your learning. There may have been a moment when you successfully identified a discrepancy or streamlined a process. These small victories are stepping stones to greater confidence and proficiency.

Boosting confidence in bookkeeping requires practical strategies. Practice new skills in a low-pressure environment, such as a mock business setup or a simplified version of your records. This approach allows you to experiment and learn without fearing real-world consequences. Set small, achievable goals to build momentum. For instance, aim to reconcile accounts weekly or categorize a specific number of daily transactions. Each completed task fuels your confidence, reinforcing your ability to manage more complex bookkeeping challenges. These incremental successes accumulate, transforming your perception from uncertainty to self-assurance.

Continuous practice is the key to mastering any skill, and bookkeeping is no exception. Regular practice reinforces what you've learned and builds a muscle memory of sorts. Engage in daily bookkeeping exercises, even just a few minutes each day. The repetition solidifies your understanding and enhances your efficiency. Simulating real-world scenarios, such as preparing for tax season or managing a sudden influx of transactions, can further boost your readiness. These simulations prepare you for actual challenges, providing a safe space to apply what you've learned and identify areas for improvement.

Motivational success stories can be powerful catalysts for confidence. Consider the story of a self-taught bookkeeper who, through perseverance, landed their first client. Initially plagued by self-doubt and lacking formal training, they committed to daily practice and sought mentor feedback. Each client interaction built their confidence, eventually leading to a thriving bookkeeping business. Or think of an entrepreneur who faced an initial bookkeeping challenge when their business began to grow. Instead of shying away, they embraced the challenge, dedicating time each week to refine their skills. Over time, they managed their finances and began advising others, transforming a challenge into an opportunity for growth.

Interactive Element: Self-Assessment Checklist

To support your confidence-building journey, use this self-assessment checklist:

- **Evaluate Current Skills**: Reflect on your strengths and areas for improvement.
- **Set Personal Benchmarks**: Define specific goals for skill enhancement.
- **Identify Past Successes**: Recognize moments of achievement and learning.
- **Prepare for Challenges**: Simulate real-world scenarios to build readiness.
- **Celebrate Milestones**: Acknowledge progress and use it to fuel further motivation.

You'll grow your confidence by consistently applying these strategies and drawing inspiration from those who have successfully navigated their paths. Each step forward, no matter how small, is a testament to your capabilities and potential. As you continue to engage with book-keeping, remember that confidence is not a destination but a journey. It's about embracing the process, learning from every experience, and using those lessons to empower yourself and your business.

9.2 CULTIVATING A POSITIVE MONEY MINDSET

Imagine money as a versatile, powerful tool that, when used wisely, can build dreams, forge opportunities, and create lasting security. This perspective shifts how you approach financial decisions. It's not about fear or scarcity but about potential and growth. A positive money mindset doesn't come from having abundant wealth but from viewing money as a means to achieve your goals. It allows you to see beyond the immediate constraints, focusing instead on the opportunities money can unlock. This transformative mindset alters how you make financial choices, set goals, and respond to challenges. With a growth-oriented perspective, you look at financial setbacks not as insurmountable obstacles but as learning experiences that pave the way for future success.

Developing this mindset involves more than just positive thinking. It requires cultivating a habit of gratitude for what money has already helped you achieve. By acknowledging your financial accomplishments, no matter how small, you reinforce a sense of abundance. This gratitude translates into setting positive financial affirmations. These affirmations are not mere wishful thinking but deliberate statements that shape your financial behavior. They build confidence, reduce anxiety, and focus your energy on constructive outcomes. For instance, affirming that "I am capable of managing my finances effectively" can shift your daily actions and decisions toward more responsible financial management.

Consider the story of an entrepreneur who faced financial struggles early in their career. By changing their money mindset, they transformed these challenges into stepping stones. Instead of viewing limited resources as a hindrance, they saw them as a chance to innovate and streamline operations. This shift led to a breakthrough, where the entrepreneur's business survived and thrived, eventually expanding into new markets. Similarly, a personal finance turnaround might involve an individual rethinking their relationship with debt. By adopting a positive money mindset, they gradually reduced their liabilities, increased savings, and improved their credit score. These transformations highlight how a change in perspective can lead to tangible financial success.

To foster this mindset, engage in activities that encourage a constructive approach to money. Start by journaling about your financial goals and achievements. This practice helps clarify your objectives and track your progress, reinforcing positive habits. Use visualization exercises to focus on financial success. Picture yourself achieving your goals, whether paying off debt, saving for a home, or investing in your business. This mental imagery reinforces your commitment and motivates you to take actionable steps.

Visual Element: Money Mindset Reflection Journal

Consider maintaining a reflection journal to support your money mindset journey. Use it to record:

- **Financial Goals**: Define short-term and long-term objectives.
- **Achievements**: Note milestones and successes, reinforcing positivity.
- **Affirmations**: Write daily affirmations that focus on financial growth.
- **Reflections**: Capture thoughts on how changing your mindset impacts decisions.

This journal serves as a tangible reminder of your growth, helping you stay focused and motivated. As you cultivate a positive money mindset, you'll find that financial challenges become less daunting and opportunities for growth more apparent. This change in mindset enables you to make choices that support your goals, paving the way for greater financial success and personal fulfillment.

9.3 CONTINUOUS LEARNING AND IMPROVEMENT IN BOOKKEEPING

In the ever-evolving bookkeeping landscape, the importance of life-long learning cannot be overstated. Staying updated with new industry trends and best practices is crucial for maintaining relevance in your field. Imagine the world of bookkeeping as a dynamic ocean; its currents constantly shift with emerging technologies and regulatory changes. To navigate these waters successfully, you must be willing to learn and adapt continually. For instance, embracing new technologies and methodologies can streamline your bookkeeping processes, making them more efficient and less prone to errors. This adaptability not only benefits your current operations but also prepares you for future challenges that may arise. By actively seeking new information and skills, you ensure that your bookkeeping practices remain sharp and effective.

To facilitate this ongoing education, there are numerous resources available that can support your growth. Online courses and certifications provide a convenient way to deepen knowledge and acquire new skills. These courses often cover various topics, from basic bookkeeping principles to advanced software applications, allowing you to tailor your learning to your needs. Additionally, networking events and professional associations offer opportunities to connect with other bookkeeping professionals. These gatherings can be invaluable for sharing insights, learning about industry developments, and finding mentorship. Engaging with a community of peers also provides moral support and motivation, reminding you that you are not alone in your pursuit of excellence.

Regular skill enhancement offers tangible benefits that extend beyond personal satisfaction. By continuously learning, you can improve the efficiency and effectiveness of your bookkeeping processes. This growth enables you to adapt to changes in financial regulations, ensuring compliance and avoiding potential legal complications. Moreover, staying informed about industry trends enhances your decision-making skills, allowing you to make more strategic choices that can positively impact your business or career. For instance, understanding new tax laws or accounting standards can help you confidently navigate complex financial situations, ultimately leading to better outcomes.

Embracing the learning process is crucial for building resilience and confidence in your bookkeeping abilities. Celebrating milestones and achievements along the way reinforces your progress and encourages you to keep pushing forward. Whether mastering a new software program or successfully managing a complicated financial report, each accomplishment is a testament to your dedication and perseverance. Viewing challenges as learning opportunities rather than obstacles shifts your perspective and empowers you to approach difficulties proactively. This outlook fosters a sense of empowerment and autonomy, enabling you to take ownership of your professional development.

Consider the story of a bookkeeper who started their career with modest beginnings but rose to the position of Chief Financial Officer (CFO) through continuous learning and dedication. Initially, they focused on mastering the basics, but as they gained experience, they sought advanced training and certifications. This commitment to growth expanded their skill set and opened doors to new opportunities and responsibilities. Their journey demonstrates the transformative power of education and its ability to propel careers to new heights. Similarly, a small business owner who invested in improving their bookkeeping skills saw significant improvements in their company's financial health. By implementing best practices and staying informed about industry trends, they were able to streamline operations, reduce costs, and increase profitability. These examples highlight the profound impact that continuous learning can have on personal and professional success.

9.4 THE FUTURE OF BOOKKEEPING: TRENDS AND INNOVATIONS

The future of bookkeeping is shaped by rapid technological advancements, altering the landscape in ways we couldn't have imagined a decade ago. Take artificial intelligence and machine learning, for example. These technologies are not just buzzwords; they are actively transforming how we handle data. AI can analyze vast amounts of information quickly, identifying patterns and trends that might take a human hours or even days to uncover. This capability is beneficial in predictive analytics, where AI can forecast financial outcomes based on historical data. Imagine a business predicting its cash flow weeks in advance with remarkable accuracy, allowing for better planning and decision-making. Machine learning algorithms continue to learn and improve, making predictions more precise over time, thus offering bookkeepers a powerful tool to enhance their financial management capabilities.

Blockchain technology, often associated with cryptocurrencies, is another game-changer for bookkeeping. Its potential for secure transactions is immense. Using a decentralized ledger, blockchain ensures that every transaction is transparent and tamper-proof. This level of security is invaluable, especially in sectors where data integrity is critical. For instance, a company implementing blockchain for its financial transactions can significantly reduce the risk of fraud and errors. Each transaction is recorded in a way that cannot be altered, providing an unchangeable audit trail. This feature boosts trust and streamlines auditing processes, saving time and resources. As blockchain technology becomes more mainstream, its applications in bookkeeping are likely to expand, offering even more innovative solutions for financial professionals.

The impact of digital transformation on bookkeeping is profound, reshaping how we access and manage data. Cloud-based solutions, for instance, provide real-time access to financial information from anywhere in the world. This accessibility is crucial for businesses with remote teams or multiple locations. Imagine generating financial reports on the go without being tethered to a specific device or location. Cloud solutions also facilitate collaboration, allowing team members to work together seamlessly, regardless of where they are. This flexibility enhances productivity and ensures everyone can access the most up-to-date information, reducing the likelihood of errors and miscommunications.

Automation is another pillar of digital transformation, revolutionizing routine bookkeeping tasks. Tasks that once required hours of manual input can now be completed in a fraction of the time. Automation tools handle everything from data entry to invoice processing, freeing bookkeepers to focus on more strategic activities. This shift boosts efficiency and reduces the risk of human error, leading to more accurate financial records. As automation technology evolves, its integration into bookkeeping processes will become even more seamless, further enhancing productivity and accuracy.

In the future, specific skills will become increasingly crucial for bookkeepers. Proficiency in data analytics and interpretation will be essential. As technologies like AI and machine learning become more ingrained in bookkeeping processes, the ability to analyze and interpret complex data sets will set successful bookkeepers apart. This skill enables financial professionals to draw meaningful insights from data, inform strategic decisions, and drive business success. Additionally, adaptability to technological advancements will be crucial. The pace of technological change is relentless, and those who can quickly adapt and integrate new tools into their workflows will thrive. This adaptability requires a mindset open to continuous learning and experimentation, allowing bookkeepers to stay at the forefront of industry developments.

Forward-thinking companies are already adopting innovative bookkeeping practices. Consider a business using AI for predictive analytics. By leveraging AI, they can accurately forecast future sales trends, allowing them to adjust inventory levels and marketing strategies proactively. This foresight leads to more efficient operations and improved profitability. Another example is a company implementing blockchain for transaction security. Using blockchain ensures that every transaction is securely recorded, reducing the risk of fraud and errors. This transparency enhances trust with stakeholders and simplifies the auditing process, saving time and resources.

As we explore these trends and innovations, it's clear that the future of bookkeeping is bright and full of possibilities. Embracing these changes will enable bookkeepers to provide greater value to their organizations, transforming how we think about and manage finances.

CONCLUSION

As we end our journey through the world of bookkeeping, I want to reflect on the profound impact this skill can have on your life and business. Throughout these pages, we've explored the fundamental principles and practical applications of bookkeeping, empowering you to take control of your financial destiny. Mastering these techniques has unlocked a door to a brighter, more secure future.

From the beginning, we emphasized the critical role bookkeeping plays in the success of any small business. It's not just about keeping records; it's about understanding the story behind the numbers. By learning how to set up a robust bookkeeping system, record transactions accurately, and interpret financial statements, you've gained the power to make informed decisions that will shape the trajectory of your business.

Each chapter has been a stepping stone on your path to financial literacy. We started by laying the groundwork and demystifying key terminology and concepts. Then, we delved into the nitty-gritty of daily bookkeeping tasks, providing time-saving techniques and strategies for staying organized. You learned how to navigate the complexities of financial statements, using them as business planning and growth tools. We tackled the intricacies of small business taxes, equipping you with the knowledge to stay compliant and maximize your deductions.

But this book is about more than just technical skills. It's about empowerment. It's about the confidence that comes from understanding your finances inside and out. No longer will you feel intimidated by numbers or uncertain about your business's financial health. You now possess the tools to take charge, make proactive choices, and steer your enterprise toward success.

I want you to know that this is just the beginning of your journey. The world of bookkeeping is constantly evolving, with new technologies and best practices emerging constantly. Embrace the opportunity to keep learning, stay curious, and adapt your skills to the changing landscape. By committing to continuous improvement, you'll stay ahead of the curve and discover new ways to streamline your processes and boost your bottom line.

As you close this book, I encourage you to implement your newfound knowledge. Start implementing the strategies we've discussed, whether setting up a chart of accounts, automating your expense tracking, or analyzing your financial reports for insights. The more you practice, the more natural these tasks become until bookkeeping feels like second nature.

Remember, too, that your mindset matters. Approach bookkeeping not as a chore but as an opportunity to gain clarity and control over your financial life. Celebrate your successes, learn from your challenges, and maintain a positive outlook. With the right attitude, you'll find that bookkeeping can be a source of empowerment and even enjoyment.

Finally, I congratulate you on making it to this point. By investing in your financial education, you've taken a significant step toward securing your future. You should be proud of your dedication and discipline in mastering these critical skills. As you embark on the next phase of your journey, know that you have the knowledge and tools to navigate whatever challenges come your way.

So, go forth with confidence. Embrace the power of bookkeeping to transform your business and your life. And remember, you're not alone in this journey. As a seasoned accounting and bookkeeping expert, I'm always here to support and guide you. Together, we can build a future where financial literacy is the norm, small businesses thrive, and individuals like you are empowered to achieve their dreams.

Keep learning, keep growing, and most importantly, keep believing in yourself. The world of financial success is yours for the taking, one well-balanced book at a time

BIBLIOGRAPHY

- *Stock Market Basics For Beginners - Cancreatewealth.com.* https://cancreatewealth.com/tag/stock-market-basics-for-beginners/
- *The Importance of Bookkeeping in Business - Accounting - KPI* https://www.kpi.com/en/importance-of-book-keeping/#:~:text=Bookkeeping%20is%20important%20for%20businesses%20for%20several%20reasons%2C%20including%20making,with%20government%20regulations%2C%20and%20offering
- *Top 10 Bookkeeping Mistakes by Small Businesses - SCORE* https://www.score.org/resource/article/top-10-bookkeeping-mistakes-small-businesses
- *Free Accounting Tools for Small Businesses* https://www.uschamber.com/co/run/finance/free-accounting-tools-for-small-businesses
- *Bookkeeping vs. Accounting: What's the Difference?* https://www.investopedia.com/articles/professionals/091715/career-advice-accounting-vs-bookkeeping.asp
- *Manual vs. Digital Bookkeeping: Pros and Cons - OpenExpert* https://openexpert.nz/finance/manual-vs-digital-bookkeeping-pros-and-cons/
- *The Best Accounting Software for Small Businesses in 2025* https://www.pcmag.com/picks/the-best-small-business-accounting-software
- *How to Start Bookkeeping: A Step-by-Step Guide* https://www.clrvw.com/how-to-start-bookkeeping-a-step-by-step-guide/
- *Top Small Business Accounting Software for 2023 - ASP* https://www.theaspteam.com/blog/top-small-business-accounting-software-for-2023
- *Best Accounting Software for Small Businesses of 2025* https://www.nerdwallet.com/p/best/small-business/accounting-software
- *Essential Steps for Accurate Transaction Recording* https://accountinginsights.org/essential-steps-for-accurate-transaction-recording/
- *Tips for saving, organizing, and finding your receipts - Microsoft* https://www.microsoft.com/en-us/microsoft-365-life-hacks/organization/tips-for-saving-organizing-and-finding-receipts
- *Debits and Credits: In-Depth Explanation with Examples* https://www.accountingcoach.com/debits-and-credits/explanation
- *Balance Sheet: Explanation, Components, and Examples* https://www.investopedia.com/terms/b/balancesheet.asp
- *How to Read a Profit and Loss Statement* https://oregonsbdc.org/how-to-read-a-profit-and-loss-statement/
- *Cash Flow Statement: What It Is and How to Read One* https://www.investopedia.com/investing/what-is-a-cash-flow-statement/
- *8 Accounting Errors to Watch Out For and How to Fix Them* https://www.brex.com/spend-trends/accounting/how-to-fix-accounting-errors-and-mistakes

- *Small Business and Self-Employed Tax Center* https://www.irs.gov/businesses/small-businesses-self-employed
- *Small Business and Self-Employed Tax Center* https://www.irs.gov/businesses/small-businesses-self-employed
- *Publication 946 (2023), How To Depreciate Property* https://www.irs.gov/publications/p946
- *The Importance of Accurate Bookkeeping for Tax Compliance* https://outoftheboxtechnology.com/blog/importance-accurate-bookkeeping-for-tax-compliance/
- *The Best Accounting Software for Small Businesses in 2025* https://www.pcmag.com/picks/the-best-small-business-accounting-software
- *Your Complete Guide to Bookkeeping for Your Business* https://www.entrepreneur.com/money-finance/your-complete-guide-to-bookkeeping-for-your-business/431193
- *15 Benefits of Cloud Accounting* https://www.netsuite.com/portal/resource/articles/accounting/cloud-accounting-benefits.shtml
- *Guide to Accounting Automation for Businesses in 2023* https://www.cpabychoice.com/post/guide-to-accounting-automation-for-businesses-in-2023
- *How To Use Financial Data To Drive Business Decisions* https://www.forbes.com/sites/melissahouston/2024/05/08/how-to-use-financial-data-to-drive-business-decisions/
- *The Importance of Regular Financial Reviews for Business ...* https://figgiesfinance.com/importance-of-regular-financial-reviews/
- *Trend Analysis - Accounting Principles II* https://www.cliffsnotes.com/study-guides/accounting/accounting-principles-ii/financial-statement-analysis/trend-analysis
- *Data-driven Decision Making for Small Businesses* https://www.databirdjournal.com/posts/data-driven-decision-making-for-small-businesses-leveraging-analytics-for-success
- *The Top 8 challenges of bookkeeping task for small retail ...* https://azbigmedia.com/business/small-business/the-top-8-challenges-of-bookkeeping-task-for-small-retail-stores/
- *17 Self-Employed Tax Deductions for Small Business ...* https://found.com/resources/common-deductions-for-freelancers
- *What Accounting System Is Best for My Service Business?* https://www.growthforce.com/blog/what-accounting-system-is-best-for-my-service-business
- *2 Bookkeeping Business Success Stories [2024]* https://www.starterstory.com/ideas/bookkeeping-business/success-stories
- *How to Build Confidence and Leadership as a Bookkeeper* https://www.thesuccessfulbookkeeper.com/blog/how-to-build-confidence-and-leadership-as-a-bookkeeper
- *How To Build A Money Mindset For Financial Success In ...* https://www.forbes.com/sites/melissahouston/2024/12/10/how-to-build-a-money-mindset-for-financial-success-in-business-and-life/

- *Best Online Bookkeeping Courses* https://www.accounting.com/degrees/bookkeeping/certificate/
- *Future of Accounting: Emerging Trends & Technologies* https://floqast.com/blog/future-of-accounting-emerging-trends-and-technologies/

www.ingramcontent.com/pod-product-compliance
Lightning Source LLC
LaVergne TN
LVHW020235210926
848481LV00016B/2214
9798349427923